# ASSESSING
## AND TREATING

# TRAUMA
# & PTSD

### SECOND EDITION

BY LINDA J. SCHUPP, PH.D.

Published by
PESI Publishing & Media
PESI, Inc
3839 White Ave
Eau Claire, WI 54703

Cover: Amy Rubenzer
Layout: Bookmasters
Editing: Marietta Whittlesey

ISBN: 978-1-55957-009-1

Printed in the United States of America

**Library of Congress Cataloging-in-Publication Data**
Schupp, Linda J. author.
  Assessing and treating trauma and PTSD / Linda J. Schupp. – 2nd edition.
    p. ; cm.
  Includes bibliographical references.
  ISBN 978-1-55957-009-1 (alk. paper) – ISBN 978-1-55957-010-7 (alk. paper)
  I. Title.
  [DNLM: 1.  Stress Disorders, Post-Traumatic.  WM 172.5]
  RC552.P67
  616.85'21–dc23
                              2015000375

PESI
Publishing
& Media
www.pesipublishing.com

# TABLE OF CONTENTS

# ACKNOWLEDGEMENTS

This book is lovingly dedicated to the memory of two significant people who profoundly influenced my life, Charles S. Adams and Linda Siler Adams, who adopted me as their very own child during the first few months of my life. They gave me all the love and nurturance an infant could ever want or need. It has been said that self-esteem is built when a child "*feels*" loved, not necessarily when a child is loved. The difference in being loved or feeling loved lies in the parent's ability to express the love in the way the child can internalize it. My precious parents were specialists in doing all the things I needed to feel loved, valued, and approved. In doing so, they gave me the priceless gift of self-worth. Had I not felt significant or whole, I might not have been able to survive the tragedies that lay ahead of me. The stability, security and essential sense of self that they lovingly constructed in me became my sails in the storms of life. If they can peek through heaven's portals, I hope they know how thankful I am that God allowed me to have such wonderful parents.

I am also indebted to Lisa Cardenas for her skill of translating illegible notes into a readable text and for her editing skills in incorporating all the new material of the 2nd edition into the manuscript. I'd like to acknowledge the current staff of PESI Publishing & Media, consisting of Linda Jackson, Hillary Jenness and Heidi Strosahl for their support and encouragement. I also want to thank Michael Olson who originally expressed the need for this book and trusted me to write it.

I would be remiss if I didn't acknowledge my many clients and friends who allowed me to walk the trauma pathway with them. Their trust in me as a co-sufferer enabled them to express the inexpressible, and brought some measure of healing, meaning, and wholeness to their lives and mine. In addition, I am ever grateful to the myriad of dedicated health care professionals who have so tirelessly given of themselves to the often unacknowledged task of "*healing the hurting.*" I applaud you for your competence, perseverance, and commitment.

# ABOUT THE AUTHOR

Linda J. Schupp, Ph.D., B.C.E.T.S. is a nationally and internationally known speaker, who has trained tens of thousands of people in her seminars. She holds a Ph.D. in psychology, an M.A. in clinical psychology, a M.Ed. in guidance and counseling, and is a board certified expert in traumatic stress. Dr. Schupp has been counseling, lecturing, and speaking for over 45 years, and is gifted at incorporating her psychological background with an entertaining flair for the humorous and dramatic.

Her past affiliations include working with master's level psychology students at Regis University which, in 1996, honored her with the prestigious "Excellence in Teaching Award." She has taught psychology to undergraduate school students at Metro State College in Denver, Colorado. Dr. Schupp has also served as adjunct faculty for The Union Institute and University Graduate College School of Professional Psychology where she worked with Ph.D. psychology students. In addition, she had the privilege of teaching psychology at St. James Bible College in Kiev, Ukraine.

Dr. Schupp maintains a private practice specializing in trauma, PTSD, depression and grief. She employs Eye Movement Desensitization Reprocessing Therapy (EMDR) as well as other trauma therapies. She has shared her trauma and grief seminars with many of the survivors and workforce personnel involved in the Oklahoma City bombing and provided counseling services to individuals affected by the Columbine High School shootings. In 2012, she taught a public seminar in Denver, Colorado and surrounding communities for all individuals who were affected by the Aurora Theater shootings.

Dr. Schupp has authored three previous books titled *False Comforters: Words That Wound, and Helps That Heal, Grief: Normal, Complicated, and Traumatic,* and the first edition of *Assessing and Treating Trauma and PTSD.* She has also produced a CD and training video titled, *Is There Life After Loss?* which is applicable for professional and lay counselors. In addition, PESI has produced numerous presentations by

Dr. Schupp: A CD—*Working with Survivors of Traumatic Stress,* a CD and DVD—*Trauma, PTSD and Grief,* and a CD and DVD—*The Spectrum of Trauma.* PESI also produced a webinar, CD, and DVD titled *Trauma, PTSD and Grief.* In 2012, Dr. Schupp produced a DVD for the American Association of Christian Counselors titled *The Experience of a Victim.* It was part of a series on crisis interventions. Dr. Schupp created videos on a variety of other topics and has made numerous radio and television appearances.

This second edition of *Assessing and Treating Trauma and PTSD* focuses on the many faces of trauma which present themselves in a multitude of disorders—some easily recognized and diagnosed, others hidden behind criteria that doesn't address the etiology of their trauma. Dr. Schupp updated all information based on the current DSM-5 as well as to add contributions of newer research and therapies.

Personally speaking, Linda has suffered the traumatic loss of her mother, father, two husbands and a son. These and other trauma-related experiences have given her a heart full of compassion and a mind filled with wisdom, which brings depth, knowledge, and understanding to the field of traumatology.

# PREFACE

Is my description of the experience of trauma purely theoretical, perhaps written from the comfortable environment of my office chair, or have I experienced any of those symptoms while residing in the *"laboratory of life?"* The theoretical understanding has been a personal journey for me and I have been imprisoned by traumatic episodes for portions of my life.

At one point in time, I had buried five out of my six immediate family members, having only my precious daughter Jackie remaining in this life. Heaven was much richer for the addition of my loved ones, but earth was poverty-stricken for me. As many wise theorists have noted in the past, it isn't just the deaths of loved ones that create great pain, it is also the horrific circumstances surrounding the deaths.

Trauma, by nature, overwhelms our capacity to endure and leaves us feeling helpless and powerless. I fully identified with such responses, and often wondered what I could do to stop the procession of untimely deaths. I was a stranger to loved ones' dying peaceful deaths from old age; all my family members were snatched from me in shocking, unexpected ways. My mother was hit by an out-of-control car circling down a spiral ramp of a parking deck, and the impact hurled her through a storefront window. She lingered unconscious for five days, then died. Later in life, my father died from a medical mistake in a nursing home. He pitifully begged the attending personnel to stop the procedure, but his cries went unheard. His heart stopped instead.

I have also experienced the untimely deaths of two husbands. The husband of my youth went to sleep at the wheel of his car, which crashed into an embankment on the side of the road and folded like an accordion. Despite the impact, there wasn't a broken bone in his body; however, the internal injuries were severe and he died before I could arrive at the hospital. Later in life, I faced the traumatic death of another husband through suicide. Upon returning home from work I found him alive, but unconscious, in our garage which was filled with fumes of carbon monoxide. Attempts to save his life were all in vain.

As traumatic as those losses were, my most severe psychological wounding occurred with a terminal diagnosis of a synovial sarcoma in the right arm of my son, Cliff. The first line of treatment was the amputation of the entire arm followed by many rounds of radiation and chemotherapy. Although he outlived the physician's projections, after six long years, a blood clot to the heart took his life.

Friends and loved ones did what they could to comfort my daughter and me, but well intentioned words and advice falls flat in the face of such trauma. At times I listened to others, and found myself wandering in the wrong direction while searching for the path to healing. Some misguided turns in the road only led to deeper despair.

The old adage, *"Physician, heal thyself"* certainly was applicable to me, and I am thankful that I can present my *"reconstructed self"* to a hurting world as a hopeful and humble survivor. Many elements contributed to my reconstruction on a physiological, cognitive, emotional, and spiritual level. During my times of intense grief, I made a conscious decision to *"search for meaning, not happiness."* Interestingly enough, happiness often follows as a byproduct. How do we receive any meaning from such senseless and devastating pain? We diligently search for it. *To redeem the grief and trauma requires one to make creative use of it.* I have determined in my present life that my tears will serve as waves of movement that thrust me forward towards others of like suffering.

Trauma creates a *"vacuum in the soul"* which can remain empty or be filled with compassion and care. I am not unique in this dedication or perseverance. Many wounded healers have gone before me, and I am simply following in their footsteps. Many trauma specialists are *"there"* because they *"have been there."* If I can ease someone's burden, shed light on the way, walk the stony pathway with them, listen to the pain and devastation of the trauma, carry them through the dangerous and treacherous hills and valleys, or simply love them through the process, then my life's journey has been a meaningful venture.

# INTRODUCTION

## WHAT CONSTITUTES A TRAUMA?

A tried and true definition of longstanding is derived from *The Penguin Dictionary of Psychology* (2009) written by A.S. Reber. He defines trauma as follows:

> *"Trauma—from the Greek work for wound, a term used freely either for physical injury caused by some direct external force or for psychological injury caused by some extreme emotional assault."*

The APA Dictionary of Clinical Psychology (2007), our most current version, provides us with the following definition:

> **Trauma** n. 1. Any disturbing experience that results in significant fear, helplessness, dissociation, confusion, or other disruptive feelings intense enough to have a long-lasting negative impact on a person's attitudes, behavior, and other aspects of functioning. Traumatic events include those caused by human behavior (e.g., rape, toxic accidents) as well as by nature (e.g., earthquakes) and often challenge an individual's view of the world as a just, safe, and predictable place. 2. Any serious physical injury, such as a widespread burn or a blow to the head.

The experience of trauma produces exhaustion on many levels. Trauma survivors are physiologically, emotionally, cognitively, and sometimes spiritually depleted. Their sympathetic nervous systems are vigilantly scanning the environment for varied stimuli, ready to fight or flee at the slightest provocation. Their inability to express or receive love, or experience positive emotions has removed any joy or meaning from their relationships. The trauma-related emotions of fear, anxiety, and depression take their toll on energy reserves. Helplessness, terror, and feelings of powerlessness and horror may become the norm. Cognitive processes may seem like the survivor is *"functioning in a fog."* Concentration, focus, and decision making can be exasperating and exhausting. If the trauma has challenged deeply held beliefs about God or philosophies about how the world should operate, then the bombardment and shattering of these security bases have left survivors in a field of desolation.

The spectra of trauma has invaded every segment of society and, because of its pervasiveness, trauma has become a multidisciplinary concern. Traumatologists predict that 70–90% of people will either witness, be exposed to, or experience a trauma sometime during their life. Trauma parades in many costumes, wearing diverse faces and occupying numerous forms, some more obvious than others. Natural disasters, combat, murders, terrorism, bombings, shootings, rapes, sexual abuse, domestic violence, and car accidents are frequent occurrences, often on public display in newspapers, television, and the media. Other trauma occurs behind closed doors and its insidious effects are evident in numerous disturbances such as borderline, antisocial, and narcissistic personality disorders, obsessive compulsive disorder, dissociative identity disorder and posttraumatic stress disorder (PTSD). Who can calculate the impact of physical and sexual child abuse that is secretive, repeated, and prolonged? The physical body of the child may survive and develop into adulthood, but the crime of *"soul murder"* may remain undetected, unpunished, and untreated.

And what about the hidden traumatic relationships that surface in our clinics or offices as depression, panic disorders, and anxiety disorders that belie the truth of their real identity as trauma? Many medical and mental health clinics, religious institutions, governmental agencies, and charitable organizations, to name a few, have heard the disguised cries of women, and sometimes men, suffering from physical, mental, emotional, verbal, financial, or sexual abuse. These victims are often so deeply traumatized that they lose their independent sense of self and bond with the perpetrator, thus continuing the cycle of abuse.

Let's look at one example of a woman with a presenting problem. Joyce explained that she had experienced trauma because her husband forgot to give her a birthday card. At first glance, some clinicians might tend to trivialize her problem but, with deeper investigation, the forgotten birthday card served as a *"trauma trigger"*. As a child, her parents celebrated her birthday by locking her in a damp, dark basement closet without food or toilet facilities and didn't release her until the next day. The forgotten birthday card had become a reminder that she was unloved and harshly dealt with as a child, and served as a reminder of earlier painful days. She feared that her husband might begin to treat her in the same horrific way. Through years of working with traumatized clients, the knowledgeable clinician will look for trauma that may be lurking behind many disorders and conditions. Trauma is the etiological agent behind many of the disorders we treat, and we must always seek it out and treat it accordingly.

What resources are available to attend to the myriad of needs that trauma victims present? What treatments are able to transform victims into survivors? Who will be there to pick up the pieces of shattered lives and reconstruct them into meaningful living? Those of us who are dedicated to the field of traumatology will arrive and respond from a multitude of occupations to fill that overwhelming need.

Treatments also present themselves from diverse theoretical orientations, providing clinicians with a vast eclectic approach. It is imperative that health care professionals avail themselves of the most current physiological and psychological approaches. To competently serve our clients, we must keep abreast of the contributions from many fields. For instance, it was previously believed that once neurons had been destroyed in the brain, they couldn't be regrown. Current neurological research has dispelled that myth and provided new understanding regarding the possibility of neuronal regrowth. Many trauma specialists are now viewing posttraumatic stress disorder and other trauma-related syndromes as neurological disorders caused by traumatic stress. Based on this neurological research, psychopharmacology has taken its proper place in the array of treatments and has much to offer. There is much research emphasizing the impact and importance of the clinician's words, facial expressions, body language and unconscious connections with the client. In addition, many therapies such as music, art, yoga, rhythms, drumming, martial arts, drama, dancing, singing, meditation and role-playing are surfacing as valid and important healing techniques. Various types of movement have proved that these forms of therapy can heal trauma on a cellular level, where talk therapies are ineffective.

Accelerated information processing also presents numerous techniques that hasten the healing and minimize the pain of trauma. Healthcare professionals can currently choose from a vast array of beneficial treatments.

Trauma has always existed and will continue to exist, so it behooves those of us in the helping professions to prepare ourselves. This book serves as a practical guide for the *"tried and true"* therapies and for the newer innovative approaches to trauma. I applaud each of you for your dedication to your particular field of service, and for your interest in the integration of traumatology with your present work. It is to be hoped that, with this multidisciplinary approach, we can make a difference in the lives of traumatized clients.

# CHAPTER ONE

# THE NATURE OF TRAUMATIC STRESS

### THE ETIOLOGY OF STRESS AND TRAUMATIC STRESS

Prior to the 1960s, the word *"stress"* was relatively unknown. Today it is a commonly used term in every avenue of life. The early research focused primarily on the effects of stress on the body. Even today, many experts consider it as a cause of disease and illness in 80% of cases. Stress can be the culprit in major situations such as cancer and heart disease and in such irritating conditions as warts. Dr. Hans Selye, a European physician and endocrinologist, coined the first definition in the 1920s to explain what he observed in his patients.

> *"Stress is the nonspecific response of the body to any demand placed upon it to adapt."*

> Hans Selye, 1956

He later refined it to include pleasurable events as well.

> *"Stress is the nonspecific response of the body to any demand placed upon it to adapt, whether that demand produced pleasure or pain."*

> Hans Selye, 1976

Lazarus offers this definition of stress:

> *"Stress occurs when an individual perceives that the demands of an external situation are beyond his or her perceived ability to cope with them".*

> Richard Lazarus, 1966/1984

Current theories have hypothesized that stress can also impact people mentally, emotionally, and spiritually.

Brian Luke Seaward (1999) reminds clinicians that Selye's definition combined with that of Richard Lazarus (1984) has been expanded by the holistic medicine field.

> *"Stress is the inability to cope with a perceived (real or imagined) threat to one's physical, mental, emotional, and spiritual well-being."*
>
> Brian Luke Seaward, 1999

Life itself cannot be lived without people experiencing stress as either a cause or an effect. A.S. Reber (2009) in *The Penguin Dictionary of Psychology* provides us with his definition:

1. Generally, any force that when applied to a system causes some significant modification of its form, usually with the connotation that the modification is a deformation or a distortion. The term is used with respect to physical, psychological, and social forces and pressures. Note that stress in this sense refers to a cause; stress is the antecedent of some effect.

2. A state of psychological tension produced by the kinds of forces or pressures alluded to in 1 above. Note that stress in this sense is an effect; stress is the result of other pressures. When meaning two is intended, the term stressor is typically used for the causal agent.

A more current definition in the *APA Dictionary of Clinical Psychology* (2007) provides the following:

> **stress** n. a state of physiological or psychological response to internal or external stressors. Stress involves changes affecting nearly every system of the body, influencing how people feel and behave. For example, it may be manifested by palpitations, sweating, dry mouth, shortness of breath, fidgeting, faster speech, augmentation of negative emotions (if already being experienced), and longer duration of stress fatigue. Severe stress is manifested in the general adaptation syndrome. By causing these mind-body changes, stress contributes directly to psychological and physiological disorder and disease and affects mental and physical health, reducing the quality of life.

Stress is sometimes viewed as either a constructive or destructive force. The difference between the two lies in the outcome. Constructive stress leads people to a better place in some facet of life without detrimental effects, while destructive stress leaves them incapacitated. For instance, Dan, a manager of a large computer firm, decided to attend an evening college class to acquire a new job skill. He temporarily felt the extra pressure during the course, but after its completion reaped the rewards of a new career promotion. In analyzing his situation, we can observe that the stress was not unduly prolonged and produced a desired result. The entrance to college may have been perceived initially as a physical and mental threat, but Dan succeeded and was no worse for the experience. Viewing constructive stress in a humorous vein, we might conclude: *"There's light at the end of the tunnel and it's not a train."* Most people need just enough tension to function at the highest level, but not so much that they break in the process.

Dr. Walter Cannon (1914), a contemporary of Hans Selye, indicated that during stress the person experiences the *"fight or flight"* syndrome. Selye (1956) coined the phrase general adaptation syndrome to explain the process which occurs. This syndrome sets the accompanying physiological, mental, and emotional arousal systems in motion. A modern, more inclusive version of Dr. Cannon's term might rename it the *"fight, flight, or freeze syndrome"* which identifies a new component. Freezing or taking an inactive, passive stance can occur in many instances in stress and traumatic stress. There are many everyday examples of a mild freezing response. For instance, Johnny doesn't move or fight back as his bigger brother bends his arm behind his back. A passive stance may prevent the further damage of a broken arm. We often observe this passivity in the animal kingdom as a small dog stops fighting and bares his throat to the conquering dog. Freezing becomes increasingly important when used as a survival mechanism in traumatic circumstances such as the child who submits to repeated sexual abuse, because the threat of a beating for non-compliance is more frightening than the abuse.

How do everyday stress responses compare with traumatic stress responses? There are clear boundary lines between the two areas. Traumatic stress is a heightened form of stress which is preceded by a trauma, an event that is considered life-threatening or life changing to self or others. Traumatic stress also occurs with multiple or repeated trauma.

Mark Lerner (2001) with the American Academy of Experts in Traumatic Stress provides a relevant definition for traumatic stress. "Traumatic stress refers to the emotional, cognitive, behavioral, and physiological experience of individuals who are exposed to, or who witness, events that overwhelm their coping and problem-solving abilities."

Bessel van der Kolk (1995) stated quite simply: *"Trauma is an inescapably stressful event that overwhelms peoples' coping mechanisms."*

Rachael Yehuda and Alexander McFarlane (1995) draw some distinctions between Selye's stress response and the PTSD experience.

> It is now clear that PTSD does provide a model for a process of adjustment and destabilization to trauma that has biological, psychological, and phenomenological dimensions. The biological investigations have demonstrated that the substrates of the disorder may not, in fact, be similar to the 'normative stress response' described by Selye, but rather may be a progressive sensitization of biological systems that leave the individual hyper-responsive to a variety of stimuli.

## THE AROUSAL ZONES

Traumatic stress, the accelerated form of stress, encompasses the total person and affects all areas of functioning. The modulation model (Ogden & Minton, 2000) demonstrates a person's ability to tolerate stress. In non-traumatic stress, whether positive or negative, the person usually remains within the optimum arousal zone (Wilbarger & Wilbarger, 1997). Bessel van der Kolk (1987) states that traumatized individuals display poor tolerance to arousal. They are unable to remain within a normal range. Dr. van der Kolk (1987) explains that the traumatized person may exist above or below the optimum arousal zone, or swing uncontrollably between the two zones. A biphasic alternation would move between hyper arousal and hypo arousal (numbing/freezing). When individuals live in either of those zones, then upper levels of processing are ineffective. Dissociation may occur. These zones contribute to two sets of defensive behaviors. Ogden (2000) states that there are hyperactive behaviors and passive responses. The Victim's Experience of Trauma checklist will clarify those two areas.

### Modulation Model

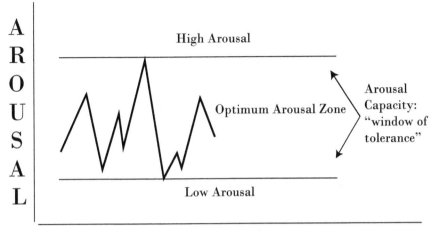

Optimum Arousal Zone

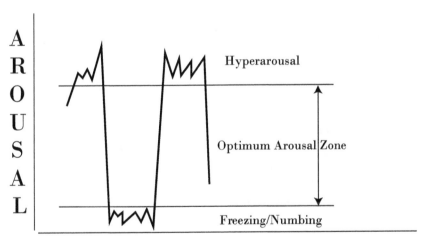

Reprinted by permission of: Ogden, P. & Kekuni, M. (2000). "Sensorimotor Psychotherapy: One Method for Processing Traumatic Memory." *Traumatology* Vol. VI, Issue 3, Article 3, Boulder, Co: Sensorimotor Psychotherapy Institute and Naropa University.

Bi-Phasic Response to Trauma

## THE VICTIM'S EXPERIENCE OF TRAUMA

I. **The Modulation Model—Optimum Arousal Zone by Dr. Pat Ogden (2000)**

   A. Normative Stress

   - High arousal = energy expenditure and the energizing effect of the sympathetic nervous system
   - Low arousal = energy conservation and the calming tranquilizing effect of the parasympathetic nervous system

**The Dividing Line Between Normative Stress and Traumatic Stress is the Experience of a Trauma.**

II. **The Bi-Phasic Response to Trauma—(You may want to use this information as a checklist for part of your intake interview.)**

   A. The **Hyper arousal** zone and some possible behaviors and disorders

Possible Behaviors or Changes:

1. Irritability _____
2. Nervousness _____
3. Exaggerated startle response _____
4. Hypervigilance _____
5. Insomnia _____
6. Nightmares _____
7. Uncontrolled rage _____
8. Violence _____
9. Dissociation _____
10. Inability to think or concentrate _____
11. Constant motion _____
12. Defensiveness _____
13. Aggressiveness _____
14. Flashbacks or re-experiencing the trauma _____

Possible Disorders:

1. Panic attack or panic disorder ⎯⎯⎯⎯⎯⎯⎯⎯⎯⎯
2. Generalized anxiety disorder ⎯⎯⎯⎯⎯⎯⎯⎯⎯⎯
3. Attention deficit hyperactivity disorder (ADHD) ⎯⎯⎯⎯
4. Learning disabilities ⎯⎯⎯⎯⎯⎯⎯⎯⎯⎯
5. Conduct disorder ⎯⎯⎯⎯⎯⎯⎯⎯⎯⎯
6. Obsessive-compulsive disorder ⎯⎯⎯⎯⎯⎯⎯⎯⎯⎯
7. Somatization disorder ⎯⎯⎯⎯⎯⎯⎯⎯⎯⎯

**B.** The **Hypo arousal** zone and some possible behaviors and disorders.

Possible Behaviors or Changes:

1. Passivity ⎯⎯⎯⎯⎯⎯⎯⎯⎯⎯
2. Submissiveness ⎯⎯⎯⎯⎯⎯⎯⎯⎯⎯
3. Inability to think or concentrate ⎯⎯⎯⎯⎯⎯⎯⎯⎯⎯
4. Dissociation ⎯⎯⎯⎯⎯⎯⎯⎯⎯⎯
5. Lack of awareness even of dangerous situations ⎯⎯⎯⎯⎯⎯
6. Lack of motivation ⎯⎯⎯⎯⎯⎯⎯⎯⎯⎯
7. Numbness ⎯⎯⎯⎯⎯⎯⎯⎯⎯⎯
8. Psychosomatic reactions ⎯⎯⎯⎯⎯⎯⎯⎯⎯⎯
9. Social isolation ⎯⎯⎯⎯⎯⎯⎯⎯⎯⎯
10. Lack of self-worth and feelings of inadequacy ⎯⎯⎯⎯⎯⎯
11. Lifeless, non-expressive mannerisms ⎯⎯⎯⎯⎯⎯⎯⎯
12. Avoidance of people, places, and activities reminiscent of the trauma ⎯⎯⎯⎯⎯⎯⎯⎯⎯⎯
13. Victim role stance ⎯⎯⎯⎯⎯⎯⎯⎯⎯⎯
14. Helplessness ⎯⎯⎯⎯⎯⎯⎯⎯⎯⎯
15. No boundaries ⎯⎯⎯⎯⎯⎯⎯⎯⎯⎯
16. Unquestioning obedience ⎯⎯⎯⎯⎯⎯⎯⎯⎯⎯
17. Repeated victim behaviors ⎯⎯⎯⎯⎯⎯⎯⎯⎯⎯
18. Inability to feel ⎯⎯⎯⎯⎯⎯⎯⎯⎯⎯
19. No defense system ⎯⎯⎯⎯⎯⎯⎯⎯⎯⎯

Possible Disorders:

**1.** Major depressive disorder _____

**2.** Persistent depressive disorder ( formerly dysthymia) _____

**3.** Dissociative disorders _____

**4.** Substance use disorder _____

**5.** Prolonged grief disorder _____

**C.** The Bi-phasic Hyper/Hypo Swing

Alterations:

The traumatized person may swing uncontrollably between the hyper- and hypo- zones exhibiting some of the behaviors from each zone.

Three Common Disorders:

**1.** Bipolar disorder _____

**2.** Acute stress disorder _____

**3.** Posttraumatic stress disorder _____

**Note:** Clinicians should exercise caution when diagnosing bipolar disorder. Frequently, a person has experienced a trauma which causes an alternation between the hyper- and hypo-arousal zones. It mimics the expressions of bipolar disorder and is treated as bipolar, but the underlying trauma has not been recognized. When the individual does not get better, a clinician may question what has happened. We should always look for a trauma before diagnosing bipolar disorder. You may find that when the trauma is treated, the symptoms of a bipolar disorder no longer exist.

## TONIC IMMOBILITY/FREEZING ANXIETY

In addition to the above checklist, we need to talk with our clients as to whether or not they experienced tonic immobility/freezing anxiety. Individuals often indicate that they were unable to move or take any action during a trauma. Sometimes people relate this to a *"deer in the headlights"* experience. This means that the animal is too stunned or terrified to move. This is also true of humans except we call it tonic immobility or freezing anxiety. We see examples of tonic immobility frequently in the animal world.

For example, I had a cat named Moppet who loved to catch field mice and present them to me as a gift. One day Moppet came trotting towards me with a tiny field mouse tightly clenched between his teeth and I was certain the mouse was dead. However, to Moppet's amazement, when he dropped the mouse at my feet, it jumped up and ran away. The smart little mouse had saved his life by remaining in a state of freezing anxiety until his release.

## MURDER AND SERENITY

Some clients have experienced the murder of a loved one or an attempt on their own life or the life of someone they love. Dr. Sherwin B. Nuland, who died in 2014, created a masterpiece in two books titled *How We Die* (1995, 2010). He has attempted to answer the question that falls from the lips of all human beings. What does it mean to die? What does a person feel during that process? This is a must-read for all clinicians.

I want to address one story from Dr. Nuland's book about a lovely nine-year-old child named Katie Mason. Katie was brutally attacked by a paranoid schizophrenic on a crowded street. He grabbed Katie, threw her down, and began viciously stabbing her face and neck. Then he sat down beside her and continued his hacking with a seven-inch hunting knife. Everyone fled and Katie and her attacker were alone. Her mother, Joan, was experiencing tonic immobility/freezing anxiety from about 20 feet away and was literally rooted by disbelief and horror. Joan's body chemistry was such that she felt the air was so thick she couldn't move through it, yet her body was warm and she felt enveloped in a mist of insulation.

Two men tried to remove the attacker and could not do so until a policeman arrived. It took the three of them to capture the crazed attacker. Joan rushed forward and took Katie in her arms despite the profuse blood covering her child. Katie's eyes were clear, almost as if she recognized her mother. It was a comfort to Joan to realize that Katie's face looked surprised, helpless and confused but not terrified. The look on Katie's face appeared as though she had released herself from pain and horror. Katie was in hypovolemic shock and died from acute hemorrhage from a severed carotid artery.

Joan repeatedly asked herself, "How much pain did Katie suffer?" Joan found comfort in understanding that endorphin elevation had spared her child from both the emotional and physical pain of a horrific death. Endorphin elevation appears to be an innate physiological mechanism that protects mammals and perhaps other animals against the emotional and physical damage of terror and pain.

The famous missionary, David Livingstone, was attacked by a lion that was intent on killing him. The lion grabbed his arm and viciously shook him until a friend shot the lion and David Livingstone was released. Mr. Livingstone stated that he felt as though he was in a dream in which there was no sense of pain or feeling of terror even though he was quite conscious of all that was happening. Although he may not have understood his body chemistry changes, he knew he had experienced a merciful provision by our benevolent Creator which lessened the pain of a potential death.

Perhaps we need to study more of Dr. Nuland's work so that we can comfort individuals who were traumatized by a near death experience or had a loved one who died a horrific death.

## STEPHEN PORGES' POLYVAGAL THEORY

Dr. Stephen Porges' polyvagal theory (2011) impacts the way we perceive our emotions, nervous system, behaviors, senses, and social self. The polyvagal theory states that the nervous system employs a hierarchy of strategies both to regulate itself and to ensure our safety when danger is present. In fact, the theme of this theory is how to remain safe in the face of danger.

Porges' (1995, 2001a, 2001b, 2004, 2005) polyvagal system (PVS) describes three hierarchical branches of the autonomic nervous system. The subsystems dictate our neurobiological reactions to activity in the environment.

1. The ventral parasympathetic vagal (VPV) branch is responsible for the wakefulness or consciousness of an individual. It turns on around social activities or in social engagements with others. It corresponds with Pat Ogden's **"optimum arousal zone."** (*See the Modulation Model.*) It is our first line of defense when we are threatened. We may try to talk our way out of a fight with an attacker for example. If that fails we move to the second subsystem.

2. The sympathetic nervous system (SNS) is the fight or flight *"energy expenditure"* system and is correlated with the adrenal glands' secreting epinephrine and norepinephrine. It is our second line of defense to enable us to *"fight or flee."* This corresponds to the hyper arousal energy expenditure system.

3. Signals from the dorsal vagal parasympathetic (DVP) branch are viewed as immobilizing and correspond to Pat Ogden's hypo arousal freezing numbing zone. This zone is concerned with decreased arousal. Sigman & Siegel, (1992) states that it leads to **"a relative decrease in heart rate**

*and respiration and accompanied by a sense of numbness"* 'shutting down within the mind' and separation from the sense of self. Hypoxia, which is a lack of oxygen in the tissues, decreases arousal. Dorsal vagal enervation enables survival-related immobilization, feigning death, behavioral shut down and synapse energy conservation. One-third of traumatized people experience the hypo arousal zone, which is triggered by lack of oxygen.

This research opens a variety of techniques and strategies for individuals that have been traumatized. We will cover that material in **Chapter 5—Treatment Techniques for Trauma**.

## PREDICTORS AND PREDISPOSITIONS TO POSTTRAUMATIC STRESS DISORDER AND TRAUMATIC STRESS

It is difficult to ascertain who are the most vulnerable or likely candidates to develop posttraumatic stress disorder (PTSD). In fact, A.S. Blank (1993) stated that it is dangerous to generalize about this population, because there are too many variables among people, the traumatic events themselves, and the circumstances surrounding the events. There is an additional problem when we limit a diagnosis to the parameters of PTSD as defined in the DSM-5. Many trauma survivors have components of a stress syndrome but do not experience the full spectrum of PTSD. Rachael Yehuda and Alexander McFarlane (1995) cite epidemiological studies of the aftermath of trauma which found that survivors can have intrusive memories of the trauma, as well as some avoidance phenomena, yet they would not meet the criteria for PTSD. They pose the theoretical question: *are there specific symptoms that differentiate people who survive a traumatic experience without being disabled from those who become severely symptomatic?* Much research is still attempting to answer this question.

Differences of opinion existed even among the early researchers. Edouard Stierlin (1901, 1911), a Swiss psychiatrist, was the first researcher to study a non-clinical population's reaction to disaster. After the 1907 earthquake in Messina, Italy which killed 70,000 of its inhabitants, he observed that no previous psychopathological predisposition was required to render a *traumatic neurosis* diagnosis. The event itself was quite sufficient to produce great psychological distress. Bonhoeffer (1926), a German psychiatrist, totally disagreed with Stierlin and felt that traumatic neurosis wasn't an illness but a means to acquire compensation from the government.

However, he did think certain individuals were predisposed to what he termed *"compensation neurosis."*

Arieh Y. Shalev (1996) summarized 38 studies which focused on five primary influences that predicted whether or not a victim developed PTSD.

1. Pre-trauma vulnerability
2. Magnitude of the stressor
3. Preparedness for the event
4. Quality of the immediate and short-term responses
5. Post event "recovery" factors

As with every physical or mental condition, the outcome will vary from one client to another. Many variables that are interwoven within the fabric of the person affect the prognosis. Most theorists, researchers, and trauma specialists unanimously believe that *"dose-response"* is an accurate predictor of who will develop some form of traumatic stress. The experience could be sexual abuse, rape, natural disaster, terrorism, domestic violence, combat, accidents, or other traumas, but the common denominator is the dose response. The greater the exposure to horrific sights, sounds, smells, tastes and tactile stimuli as well as the threat to one's life, the more likely the person will develop PTSD or some other trauma-related condition. It is safe to conclude that individuals who are directly exposed to dangerous life-threatening events have the highest risk of suffering traumatic stress effects.

Most theorists and clinicians believe that pre-existing psychiatric/ psychological conditions or biological factors could increase vulnerability. Friedman (2001) indicates that gender is also a factor. He explains that women are twice as likely to develop PTSD as men probably because women have experienced more interpersonal abuse where there has been a human perpetrator. This type of abuse, particularly repeated abuse, is a more accurate predictor of PTSD than the impersonal or impartial traumatic effects of natural disasters. Age at which a trauma occurs is another variable. For instance, child abuse in any form such as physical, sexual, verbal, economic, or separation from a parent sets one up for PTSD or for what Judith Herman (1992) termed complex PTSD. Young adults under age 25 who have experienced a trauma are also at risk. Even genetics seems to predispose one to PTSD or to protect from it. Of course, a diagnosis of acute stress disorder (ASD) could serve as a predictor since 83% of ASD sufferers develop PTSD (Brewin, et al., 1999). Veterans of war who witnessed or participated in atrocities have increased risk, as do civilians and children who were involved in war experiences. There are some studies which show that those without a college education are also at increased risk. Of course, previous trauma experiences prior to the current one would predispose the individual to PTSD, as well as damaging life circumstances such as deaths of loved ones, job loss, financial problems, or divorce.

Kessler, et al. (1995) have shown that 8% of people living in the United States have suffered with PTSD due to such traumas as childhood abuse, natural disasters, car accidents, rapes, assault, and a variety of additional traumas. Bremner (2002) states that *"16% of women are sexually abused before their 18th birthdays, and about half as many men, which means that about 50 million individuals in this country were severely abused in childhood."* Bremner, Vermetten, and Mazure (2000) have revealed in their research that emotional abuse and neglect may be as damaging as sexual abuse.

Mark Friedman (2001) states that approximately 40% of PTSD sufferers will not recover even if they receive treatment. This doesn't mean they haven't shown improvement, but that the disorder will remain throughout their lifetime in a severe chronic state. Some clinicians disagree with this percentage, and with new treatments and medications, perhaps many more will be helped. Regardless of the percentages, there will be those clients who will have some degree of impairment throughout their lives.

## "HIGH-RISK" INDICATORS FOR POSTTRAUMATIC STRESS DISORDER (PTSD)

Dr. Mark D. Lerner of The American Academy of Experts in Traumatic Stress (2001) provides us with the following list of potential indicators for PTSD. You may choose to use this information as a checklist for your clients.

_____prior exposure to severe adverse life events (e.g., combat)

_____prior victimization (e.g., childhood sexual and physical abuse)

_____significant losses

_____close proximity to the event

_____extended exposure to danger

_____pre-trauma anxiety and depression

_____chronic medical condition

_____substance involvement

\_\_\_\_\_history of trouble with authority (e.g., stealing, vandalism, etc.)

\_\_\_\_\_mental illness

\_\_\_\_\_lack of familial/social support

\_\_\_\_\_having no opportunity to vent (i.e., unable to tell one's story)

\_\_\_\_\_strong emotional reactions upon exposure to the event, physically injured, etc.

### Other Predictors

\_\_\_\_\_dose-response

\_\_\_\_\_gender—women twice as likely as men

\_\_\_\_\_age—childhood, young adults under 25

\_\_\_\_\_genetics—degrees of resiliency

\_\_\_\_\_diagnosis of acute stress disorder (ASD)

\_\_\_\_\_war experiences—involved civilians and children

\_\_\_\_\_veterans of War—witnessed or participated in atrocities

\_\_\_\_\_lack of college education

\_\_\_\_\_previous trauma

\_\_\_\_\_dissociation

\_\_\_\_\_suicidal ideation

\_\_\_\_\_sense of failure

\_\_\_\_\_feelings of defectiveness or shame

## DSM-5® PREDICTORS FOR PTSD

The DSM-5 divides the risk factors for developing PTSD into three categories: *pre-traumatic, peri-traumatic* and *posttraumatic*. The *pre-traumatic* factors include temperamental issues. They might include childhood emotional problems before age six, (e.g., a prior traumatic exposure, externalizing or anxiety problems) and prior mental disorders (e.g., obsessive compulsive disorder, panic disorder, PTSD, or depressive disorder). These temperamental factors could result in an obvious risk factor for developing PTSD with the current traumatic event. Secondly, we should consider environmental factors as well. Has this individual experienced any of the following: lower socioeconomic status, lower education level, previous trauma, family dysfunction or family psychiatric history, cultural characteristics, lower intelligence, racial/ethnic status, or other environmental stressors? In addition, DSM-5 states that we should consider the genetic and physiological impact. Females and younger children are more susceptible at the time of exposure to a trauma. Certain genotypes may either be protective or may increase risk after exposure to traumatic events. Obviously, social support prior to a trauma is definitively protective.

*Peri-traumatic* factors would certainly take environmental considerations into account. It has been said many times by other researchers that the *"dose response"* is a gigantic issue. In other words, the severity of the trauma and the intake of sights, sounds, smells, etc. becomes a significant predictor. DSM-5 states, *"the greater the magnitude of trauma, the greater likelihood of PTSD"* (APA, 2013). Examples of such severe traumas would include trauma perpetrated by a caregiver or that involving a witnessed threat. For military personnel, we might consider killing an enemy, witnessing atrocities, or being a perpetrator as obvious risk factors. Dissociation itself that occurs during and after a trauma certainly poses a risk factor.

There are two primary *posttraumatic* risk factors. The first is temperament as mentioned among pre-traumatic factors. It would also involve negative appraisals, inappropriate coping strategies, and perhaps the development of acute stress disorder. We know that 83% of individuals who develop acute stress disorder move on to develop full blown PTSD. The second primary risk factor is environmental, which would involve repeated upsetting reminders, often known as *"trauma triggers"*. It would also be detrimental for a person to experience an adverse life event, have financial losses, or experience trauma-related losses after encountering a horrendous trauma. Lack of social or family support for adults or children also sets them up for development of PTSD.

The risk for developing PTSD, and its expression, differs across cultural groups. It behooves clinicians to understand the culture of their clients. Some risk is determined by the type of traumatic exposure such as genocide, the meaning attributed to the traumatic event, the inability to perform ritualistic funeral rites after a mass killing, the ongoing sociocultural context such as residing among unpunished perpetrators in post-conflict settings or perhaps acculturative stress in immigrants. Religious expressions as well as religious persecutions for perpetrators are different across cultural groups. Some groups may experience avoidance and numbing symptoms, distressing dreams and somatic symptoms such as dizziness, shortness of breath, or heat sensations. Each culture may have its own manner of expressing or not expressing the trauma. Each culture must be studied accordingly, because these individuals will have different behavioral and cognitive templates.

PTSD is more prevalent among females than males over the entire lifespan. Females also experience PTSD for a longer period than do males. The increased risk for females may be attributable to more exposure to traumatic events such as rape and interpersonal violence. In certain populations which are accustomed to such stressors, the gender differences are nonsignificant.

Traumatic events, such as childhood abuse, increase a person's suicide risk. A clinician should also look for suicidal ideation and suicide attempts. When a person is diagnosed with PTSD, they eventually may make a suicide plan or actually attempt suicide.

## THE BRAIN, BODY, AND MIND CONNECTION

Bessel van der Kolk et al. (1994) explains that the *"brain, body, and mind are inextricably linked, and it is only for heuristic reasons that we can still speak of them as if they constitute separate entities. Alterations in any one of these three will ultimately affect the other two."*

Dr. Douglas Bremner (2002) provides us with a summary regarding the inter-relatedness of the mind, brain, and body in respect to traumatic experiences:

> "Up until now, there has been a false dichotomy between physical and mental disease. It is artificial to separate mind and brain, physical and mental, and that the effects of psychological trauma on the individual needs to be considered in neurological terms. The same processes stimulated by stress responses that may lead to depression and behavioral changes are mediated by stress responsive systems like cortisol and catecholamine that also have effects on physical health such as heart disease and infection."

Bremner (2002) states that what an individual *"sees, hears, smells, and feels"* then travels through perceptions and is modified by prior memories, emotions, and beliefs. It then is processed by the nervous system and becomes a neurological response and a new set of memories and cognitions. He continues to explain that these events have *"effects on cardiovascular, immunological, and metabolic function."*

What does this information mean to the myriad health care professionals who treat trauma? The answer is simple; these professionals must envision the entire scope of the impact of trauma. Tunnel vision doesn't work; a more comprehensive approach must be employed if the client is properly treated.

A holistic model of health should be adopted where we provide a network of referrals to our clients so that the whole person is addressed. For instance, a mental health counselor working with a survivor of traumatic stress would ensure that the client has an existing network of medical professionals who are aware of and working on the physiological aspects of the trauma. The reverse is also true where medical professionals can refer a client to mental health professionals. If diverse occupations remain isolated and focus only on their specialty, then the client is not truly served and total healing may not occur. Isolation in our occupations is an injustice to our clients.

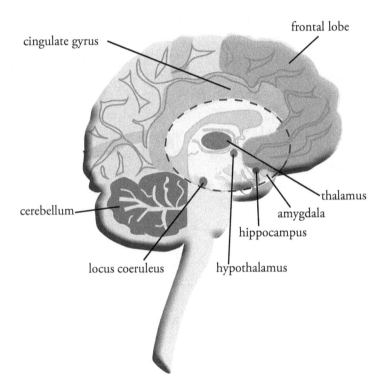

## THE LIMBIC SYSTEM "EMOTIONAL BRAIN"

It is helpful to know the various components of the brain that affect our emotions after experiencing a traumatic event.

### Amygdala

This almond shaped structure which consists of the right amygdala and the left amygdala, one in each hemisphere, is synonymous with the term *"emotional memory."* It is part of the limbic system in the temporal lobe and plays an important role in emotional behavior, particularly aggressive and fear behaviors. The amygdala assists in memory functions also, as well as in motivation. Le Chapman, et al. (1954), Le Doux (1993), and Davis (1992) have shown that the amygdala regulates fear and other emotional responses, and prolonged traumatic stress affects the ability of the amygdala to recognize a real threat. It evokes an over-abundance of the fear response to non-threatening events resulting in a *"startle response"* and a continuing arousal state.

For these reasons, the amygdala is the primary mediator of PTSD symptoms and is a sophisticated and many-faceted structure which appreciates flavors of desired foods, as well as the sights or cooking sounds of foods. The amygdala also reads people as to whether they are making pleasant sounds or angry ones, or demonstrating frightening or pleasant faces. This organ produces large amounts of endorphins sometimes known as painkillers and benzodiazepines, which can be tranquilizing like the drugs by that name. It is also involved in activities that range from emotions, phobias, traumatic responses, flashbacks, rage, anger, aggression, sexuality and endocrine functions.

In regard to everyday life and to trauma, the amygdala is the most important part of the brain for expression of emotional responses that are provoked by negative stimuli. The amygdala learns the significance of external events, and aids in processing highly charged memories like terror and horror. It is active during a traumatic event and while remembering a traumatic event. Damage to the central nucleus of the amygdala reduces or eliminates emotions and physiological responses. Experiments have been conducted in which the amygdala of individuals with sociopathic tendencies is obliterated, and they become pleasant, passive and flat in their emotional expressiveness.

Flashbacks and re-experiencing of the trauma, along with nightmares of the event, are mediated by the amygdala. The amygdala sends false alarms alerting the person to danger when there is none. Any stimuli that are vaguely reminiscent of, or remotely connected to, the trauma that was experienced can cause the amygdala to react. A trauma trigger is a reminder of the traumatic event. For example, when a car backfires, it could remind a war veteran of gunfire in battle. Because of these trauma triggers, the person relives or feels exactly as though the trauma was being re-enacted. These events cause great distress for the traumatized person and trauma triggers can occur when least expected.

## Hippocampus

The hippocampus is a seahorse shaped organ, which is present in both hemispheres of the brain. It is involved with *"declarative memory,"* which is that which can be declared, stated or told in words. It is also involved in short-term memory, held temporarily, and moved to long-term or forgotten. The hippocampus ties all the pieces of the trauma together. The hippocampus is closely aligned with the amygdala and receives information from it, which then the hippocampus puts into context. It also receives information from all regions of the sensory association cortex, which is responsible for abstract thought and language. Bremner (2002) explains that the hippocampus puts memories into a timeline, weighs them and puts them into perspective. The hippocampus can't function well during a traumatic threat. It shuts down, and the emotions take over. Its usual assistance in processing and storing an event is not available. The hippocampus gives events a beginning, middle and end. Regarding PTSD, one of its features is a sense that the trauma hasn't ended.

Cortisol is a hormone released by the cortex (outer portion) of the adrenal gland when a person is under stress. Damage to the hippocampus by high levels of cortisol disrupts its ability to form new memories. In fact, too much cortisol can cause atrophy or cell death in the hippocampus. The hippocampus experiences brain cell death due to high levels of cortisol, or through some other means, the person may have significant memory problems or may experience a change in their identity, or perhaps use dissociation in a variety of forms.

Because of an overabundance of cortisol, the 5-HT1A protein receptor bindings have died, depleting the hippocampus of serotonin, thus leading to anxiety, depression, and PTSD symptoms. The good news is that neurogenesis can occur, and the selective serotonin reuptake inhibitor (SSRI) medications have been shown to work to produce new brain cells. The hippocampus puts memories into a timeline, weighs them and puts them into perspective. The hippocampus can't function well during a traumatic threat. It shuts down and the emotions take over. Its usual assistance in processing and storing an event is not available. The hippocampus gives events a beginning, middle and an end. Regarding PTSD, one of its features is a sense that the trauma hasn't ended, Bremner (2002).

### Frontal Lobe

The frontal lobe, another important area of the brain, deserves attention in regard to psychological trauma, since it is highly sensitive to stress. The frontal cortex is occupied with planning, evaluating, organizing, and executing; the frontal lobe is also involved in mood regulation and emotion. The medial prefrontal cortex generates primitive fear reactions and also sorts and sifts real from imaginary threats, so we can respond accurately. In prolonged stress, the medial prefrontal cortex malfunctions and cannot tell us which fears pose a real threat and which do not. This inability sets up an unregulated fear response that keeps PTSD clients in a hyper vigilant state.

### Cingulate Gyrus

The cingulate gyrus runs longitudinally through the central deep aspects of the frontal lobes. It allows us to shift attention from one thing to another and to think about one idea and then to move on to another idea. Dr. Daniel Amen (1998) states: ***"This part of the brain is cognitive flexibility."*** You can focus and concentrate on one area of thought, then focus and concentrate on something else. If the cingulate gyrus is impaired or overactive, this cognitive flexibility is diminished. This organ also regulates a cooperative spirit. If it works effectively, it's easy to behave in a cooperative manner. If it is not functioning properly, the person may experience lack of impulse control.

### Thalamus

The thalamus is a structure of two egg-shaped masses of walnut sized tissue sitting at the top of the brain stem. It is an important relay center for sensory information flowing into the brain, and is connected to all parts of the brain. It can be considered the gateway from the outside of the brain to the inside. It functions like a good secretary who receives important information and passes it on to all who need it. The thalamus receives information from different sense organs and acts as a filter, selecting only information of particular importance from the mass of sensory signals it receives. Obviously, if danger is on the horizon, it quickly sends a signal to the limbic structures so they can ready the individual for the attack.

### Hypothalamus

The hypothalamus is roughly the size of a cherry and sits behind the eyes and beneath the thalamus in the forebrain. It has nerve connections to most regions of the nervous system, and maintains overall control over the sympathetic nervous system, which manages the internal body organs. With regard to trauma, when we are frightened or alarmed, some part of the brain sends signals to the hypothalamus to turn on the *"fight or flight system"* which causes a faster heartbeat, increased breathing, widening of the pupils of the eyes, increased blood flow to muscles and release of epinephrine and norepinephrine. It also controls the hypothalamic pituitary adrenal system, which controls the amount of cortisol that is released during prolonged trauma. In addition, the parasympathetic nervous system works under the guidance of the hypothalamus. Its primary neurotransmitter is acetylcholine, and it produces a calming, tranquilizing state. This system has a calming effect when we are in a resting state and does a balancing act throughout the day with the arousing sympathetic nervous system.

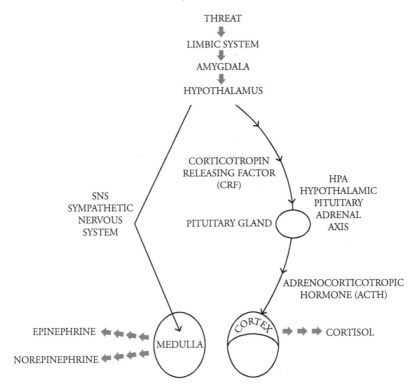

## Response to Trauma

THREAT

LIMBIC SYSTEM

AMYGDALA

HYPOTHALAMUS

CORTICOTROPIN RELEASING FACTOR (CRF)

SNS SYMPATHETIC NERVOUS SYSTEM

HPA HYPOTHALAMIC PITUITARY ADRENAL AXIS

PITUITARY GLAND

ADRENOCORTICOTROPIC HORMONE (ACTH)

EPINEPHRINE

NOREPINEPHRINE

MEDULLA

CORTEX

CORTISOL

## NEUROBIOLOGICAL CHANGES IN THE BRAIN

Current research has proven that traumatic stress can have detrimental effects on brain structure and function. Bremner (2002) has conducted extensive research on the neurological effects of extreme stress. He reminds us that:

> The brain areas most sensitive to stress are the same systems that we call upon for survival in a situation of extreme threat, such as the norepinephrine and cortisol systems. These brain areas are very sensitive to the effects of stress. Traumatic stressors have neurological consequences that in turn mediate symptoms of stress-related psychiatric disorders like PTSD and depression. Brain areas involved in memory also play a critical role in the stress response.

Walter Cannon's (1927) fight or flight syndrome provides a picture of the kinds of stress-related responses a person might employ. If a threat is conveyed from the amygdala to the hypothalamus, then the hypothalamus sets the fight or flight response in motion. Whenever we encounter a threat to our life, be it human, animal, or inanimate object, our body releases enormous amounts of epinephrine, norepinephrine, and cortisol to provide the energy to fight or flee. The locus coeruleus in the brain stem also floods the brain with norepinephrine to provide increased alertness and ability to act. Neurological researchers agree that we need those chemicals for survival, but too much of them negatively affect the brain, causing it to malfunction. With long-term traumatic stress, these systems keep pumping out too much of these stimulants and don't shut down when the threat has abated.

Cortisol, one of the survival chemicals, rearranges the distribution of our energy to assist with prolonged stress. Bremner (2002) states that it increases our heart rate, raises our blood pressure, provides oxygen and strength to the muscles and brain, supplies more serum glucose, causes free fatty acid coagulation, and enhances blood coagulation ability, to name a few of the essential physiological changes.

Bremner (2002) explains that elevated levels of cortisol can damage the hippocampus, the structure in the limbic cortex of the temporal lobe, which is involved in learning and memory. Elevated cortisol also affects mood which leads to depression and feelings of fatigue. McEwen, et al. (1992), Sapolsky, (1996), and Uno, et al., (1989) have also conducted studies that clearly substantiate the negative effects of stress-released cortisol on the brain.

In addition, Robert Sapolsky's experiments on monkeys also revealed that severe stress damages the hippocampus, causing problems with memory. Bremner (2002) reiterates that, *"stress may have resulted in damage to the hippocampus in PTSD patients, and that this could explain the memory problems . . ."* He noted that his PTSD patients had problems with new learning and current memory tasks, yet past memories prior to PTSD were intact. These individuals demonstrated similarities to patients suffering from what Bremner termed *neurological amnesia.*

Bremner, et al., (1995) found in studies with veterans diagnosed with PTSD that the hippocampus was smaller than normal; the more memory problems, the smaller the hippocampus. These findings were substantiated by magnetic resonance imaging (MRI), which clearly revealed the reduction in size of the hippocampus. Bremner, et al. (1997) also measured the size of the hippocampus in adults who were severely physically or sexually abused as children, and found the same memory problems, and a reduced hippocampus.

Stein, et al. (1997) also discovered hippocampal reductions in sexually abused women diagnosed with PTSD. Stein's work revealed that dissociative symptoms were due to hippocampus atrophy. Bremner (2002) states that in traumatized patients, the greatest decreases in volume of the hippocampus are associated with the most pronounced symptoms of dissociation. It appears that prolonged traumatic stress is the essential ingredient in structural changes of the hippocampus. This is not to say that other components are not important. Traumatic stress is frequently accompanied by depression, which also causes hippocampus volume decreases. Sheline, et al. (1996) and Bremner, Narayan, et al. (2000) attest to that finding in their research. The hippocampus also holds the memory of the emotions related to the context of the event. It is designed to protect us from further threats of a similar nature by stimulating the emotions related to the original event. Bremner (2002) noted three major problems connected to atrophy of the hippocampus: breakdowns in memory, consciousness, or identity.

McEwen, et al. (1997) reminds us that stress also decreases *"serotonin 5-HT1A receptor binding within the hippocampus."* Smith, et al., (1995) explain that neurotrophins such as brain-derived neurotrophic factor (BDNF) may be reduced in the hippocampus by stress and that decreased BDNF could cause cellular death or atrophy of the hippocampus. Until recently, it was believed that hippocampal neurons could not be regrown and the accompanying symptoms would have to be endured. The exciting news on the horizon is the possibility that the hippocampus can regrow neurons even in adults. In other words, the damage may be reversible, at least for PTSD sufferers who are no longer exposed to the stressful stimulus.

In addition to damaging the hippocampus, prolonged cortisol release may negatively impact the immune system. The early work of Hans Selye (1956/1976) suggested that this prolonged release produces the most harmful stress effects. Resick (2001) states that clients diagnosed with major depressive disorder or an anxiety disorder have elevated cortisol levels. She explains that *"the continued elevated blood sugar and metabolism spurred by cortisol will have an effect on the immune system because there is a shift away from the synthesis of proteins which are necessary for the immune system."*

Horowitz (1999) explains that the chemistry of the catecholamine, epinephrine and norepinephrine, changes during times of stress. These changes involve neural networks that *"connect the limbic, frontal cortical, basal ganglion, and hypothalamic structures."*

Disturbances in these networks and regions can disturb arousal control and alter the regulation of emotional responses (as in fright and rage attacks). The amygdala may alter its danger-recognition set points, the hippocampus its memory-encoding properties, and the medial prefrontal cortex its abilities to establish or reduce associational connections. Such disturbances may partially explain turbulent shifts in states.

## Psychopharmacological Interventions That Heal the Limbic System

1. Propranolol—can prevent PTSD if taken within 6 hours of a trauma and following a regimen of propranolol for 10 days.

2. Benzodiazepines such as Ativan, Xanax—calm the amygdala, assist with sleep and anxiety.

3. Selective serotonin reuptake inhibitors (SSRI's such as Prozac, Lexapro, Zoloft, Paxil, etc.) heal the brain and assist with anxiety, depression and posttraumatic stress disorder Prazosin or Minipress—a blood pressure medication that assists in hindering nightmares in PTSD.

## Alternative Medicine Healing Approaches for the Limbic System

1. Gamma amino butyric acid—GABA—stops panic attacks and calms brain.

2. Dilantin—an anti-seizure medication. Some alternative medicine physicians use it to calm anxiety.

3. St. John's Wort—assists with depression.

4. Vitamin B—improves overall mood, depression and anxiety.

5. Tyrosine—an amino acid building block of norepinephrine that helps with energy, focus and impulsivity.

6. Chamomile—calming and also used as sleep aid.

7. *Bacopa monnieri* with phosphatidylserine and acetyl-1-carnitine— modulates effects of stress on the brain and balances hormonal response.

8. Foods that increase serotonin levels—high carbohydrates, pastas, potatoes, bread, pastries, pretzels, popcorn.

9. Tryptophan is the natural amino acid building block for serotonin in the blood meaning more l-tryptophan can enter the brain where it is converted into serotonin. Common recommended dosage is 1,000 – 3,000 taken at bedtime. Tryptophan is also in milk, meat, especially turkey, and eggs.

10. Protein—builds brain neurotransmitters such as dopamine, serotonin and norepinephrine.

11. Inositol—a B vitamin. Inositol builds cell membranes. A recommended dosage is 12 – 20 milligrams a day.

12. Omega-3 fish oil—assists in treating depression and Bipolar disorder, and supporting cognitive function and memory.

13. Pleasant smells—particularly those that are reminiscent of happy times, heal the brain. Use various types of aromatherapy. Example: Lavender scent is calming and helpful for sleep.

14. Spend time with positive people who love you. This builds serotonin in the brain which heals emotions.

15. Animal therapy—changes brain chemistry and builds serotonin.

## PHYSICAL AND PSYCHOLOGICAL TECHNIQUES TO HEAL THE LIMBIC SYSTEM

1. Cognitive behavioral techniques—change chemistry in the brain by changing thoughts.

2. Sexual therapy heals the brain. Orgasm is like an explosion of the limbic system and releases chemicals that calm the brain. Example: An adult male with depression is asked to make passionate love with his wife. His brain calms down. Sex also causes people to bond and leads to neurochemical changes in both people.

3. The female's limbic system is larger than that of males. Because of women's larger limbic system, they are more in touch with their feelings and are better able to express themselves, thereby lowering anxiety levels.

4. Exercise allows more tryptophan to enter the brain. It is a precursor of serotonin.

5. Tai Chi assists in balancing, stabilizing, and calming the brain.

6. Eye movement desensitization reprocessing (EMDR) disconnects the horror of the trauma from the memory of the trauma.

## PATTERNS OF TRAUMA

The acceptance of PTSD as a legitimate diagnostic criterion in the DSM-III opened the door for continuing research in the study of human suffering. Controversy exists as to whether or not a psychiatric label is warranted for a condition that is a natural response to a horrific circumstance. Some theorists would prefer that it be classified as posttraumatic stress syndrome, which would remove it from the category of a mental disorder, and there is much legitimacy to that desire. On the other hand, the new DSM-5 has rewritten the criteria for PTSD and expanded it to cover areas that were not previously included in the DSM-IV-TR. Posttraumatic stress disorder is now classified in a new chapter known as Trauma- and Stressor-Related Disorders. It had previously been classified as an anxiety disorder.

Four common forms or patterns of trauma which may or may not meet the DSM criteria for PTSD have surfaced; however, all would fit under the broad umbrella of traumatic stress. They fall into categories of

1. the unexpected
2. the repetitious expected
3. the non-repetitious expected
4. the expected unexpected

The *unexpected* is often linked to a catastrophic event which probably will not be repeated. These events might include such situations as natural disasters, combat, accidents, or rape. The *repetitious expected* is an anticipated event, such as physical or sexual abuse, which is highly likely to be repeated. Victims, often women and children, may not know the exact time of the next assault but they live in a heightened state of awareness awaiting the next occurrence. The *non-repetitious expected* is a one time or singular event that is trauma-producing, but will not be repeated. The anticipated death of a child or loved one after a lingering debilitating illness, or the ultimate bedridden state of a relative caused by a degenerative disease exemplify the non-repetitious expected. The *"expected unexpected"* typifies a victim who lives in dread of a trauma, knowing that a perpetrator will produce one, yet not knowing what face and form it will take. Some domestic situations would fall into this category. For instance, Suzanne, an unemployed wife, lives with her abusive husband, Frank, and is cognizant of the likelihood of an attack, yet she doesn't know the nature of the abuse she will experience. Perhaps Frank controls her by using a variety of physical, mental, verbal, emotional, financial, sexual, and spiritual forms of abuse. Suzanne is continually off balance and can't predict even the nature of the abuse, much less the timing or frequency of its occurrence. This is a *"crazy-making"* relationship and Suzanne, if she stays, may remain in a partially dissociative state as a survival mechanism. Everyone needs some safe arenas in their lives and relationships, realms in which they feel comfortable and non-threatened. If a person feels safe in most arenas, then that individual may *"shut out"* or dissociate in the difficult ones; in other words the trauma would be compartmentalized. In this case, however, Suzanne isn't safe physically, mentally, verbally, emotionally, financially, sexually, spiritually, or any other way. She is fully feeling the effects of an ongoing *traumatic relationship*. Health care professionals may sometimes encounter clients with such relationships without identifying them as the true traumatic entity that they are.

In reality, trauma is person-specific and may not fit in any category. What is traumatic to one person may not be traumatic for another. Many varying factors determine what constitutes trauma. Helplessness and victimization are the epitome of trauma, so regulating physiological arousal, acquiring safety, and obtaining some control in life is paramount for all traumatized clients.

# CHAPTER TWO

# ASSESSMENT

Assessment serves as the first step in the development of a treatment plan for suffering clients. Clinicians need to interview, evaluate, and diagnose the specific trauma-related disorder or condition and the severity of it. The following definitions may identify some of the more common trauma-based concerns, and serve as a spring board for further analysis.

## CURRENT DEFINITIONS FOR TRAUMA-RELATED DISORDERS OR CONDITIONS

***Adjustment disorders:*** Emotional and behavioral symptoms that occur within 3 months of the onset of a stressor. These symptoms or behaviors are out of proportion to the severity or intensity of the stressor and cause significant impairment in social, occupational or other important areas of functioning. This disorder does not meet the criteria for any other mental disorder and is not an exacerbation of a preexisting mental disorder nor does it represent normal bereavement. When the stressful event and its effects have terminated, the symptoms will not persist longer than an additional 6 months (APA, 2013).

***Posttraumatic stress disorder (PTSD):*** Criteria apply to adults, adolescents, and children older than six years. PTSD involves exposure to actual or threatened death, serious injury or sexual abuse; presence of intrusive symptoms associated with the traumatic event(s), beginning after the traumatic event(s) occurred; persistent avoidance of stimuli associated

---

with the traumatic event(s), beginning after the traumatic event(s) occurred; negative alterations in cognitions and mood associated with the traumatic event(s), beginning or worsening after the traumatic event(s) occurred; marked alterations in arousal and reactivity associated with the traumatic event(s), beginning or worsening after the traumatic event(s) occurred. Duration of the disturbance is more than 1 month; the disturbance causes clinically significant distress or impairment in social, occupational, or other important areas of functioning; the disturbance is not attributable to the physiological effects of a substance (e.g., medication, alcohol) or another medical condition (APA,2013).

***Acute stress disorder:*** Requires exposure to actual or threatened death, serious injury or sexual violation in one or more of the following four ways: directly experiencing the traumatic event, witnessing in person the event, learning that the event occurred to a close family member or friend or experiencing repeated or extreme exposure to aversive details of the event. The person must experience nine symptoms from any of the following five categories: intrusion, negative mood, dissociation, avoidance, and arousal. Duration of the disturbance is three days to 1 month after the traumatic event and the symptoms typically begin immediately after the trauma but have to persist for at least three days or up to a month. The disorder causes clinically significant distress or impairment in social, occupational, or other important areas of functioning and is not attributable to physiological effects of a substance or medical condition or brief psychotic disorder (APA, 2013).

***Complex PTSD:*** A diagnostic criteria originated by Judith L. Herman, MD (1992) that was proposed but not included in the DSM-5. The responsible officials who decided what was included felt there was not enough research to warrant its inclusion. However, many clinicians use this criterion and feel that it merits our attention and the opportunity for research funding to be allocated. It deals with a *"complex form of posttraumatic stress disorder in survivors of prolonged repeated trauma."* Examples of these survivors are domestic violence victims, sexual victims, hostages, prisoners of war, concentration camp survivors, or religious cult survivors. In the DSM-IV-TR, complex PTSD would have fallen under the area titled Disorders of Extreme Stress not Otherwise Specified (DESNOS). Complex PTSD should be viewed as a distinct entity and not confused with PTSD diagnostic criteria in the DSM-IV-TR or DSM-5 (Herman, 1992).

*Generalized anxiety disorder:* Characterized by excessive anxiety and worry about numerous minor events. The intensity, duration or frequency is out of proportion to the actual likelihood or impact of the anticipated event. The person has difficulty in keeping worrisome thoughts from interfering with everyday life. It is distinguished from non-pathological anxiety by being excessive; it is more pervasive, lasts longer, and frequently occurs without any provocation (APA, 2013).

*Panic disorders:* A class of anxiety disorders characterized by recurrent panic attacks. The term is not used in cases where a known organic factor is responsible. The person may experience discrete periods of sudden onset of intense fear or terror, often associated with feelings of impending doom. During these attacks there are symptoms such as shortness of breath or smothering sensations; palpitations, pounding heart, or accelerated heart rate; chest pain or discomfort; choking; and fear of going crazy or losing control. Panic attacks may be unexpected, in which the onset of the attack is not associated with an obvious trigger and instead occurs "out of the blue," or expected, in which the panic attack is associated with an obvious trigger, either internal or external (APA, 2013).

*Phobic disorders:* A term that is equivalent to phobia. It is a persistent fear of a specific object, activity, or situation (i.e., the phobic stimulus) out of proportion to the actual danger posed by the specific object or situation that result in a compelling desire to avoid it. If it cannot be avoided, the phobic stimulus is endured with marked distress (APA, 2013).

*Bereavement:* Predominant feelings of emptiness and loss. The dysphoria in grief is likely to decrease in intensity over days to weeks and occurs in waves which are often called "pangs of grief." These waves are often associated with thoughts or reminders of the deceased or the lost object. The thought contact associated with bereavement typically includes memories of the deceased or the lost object, but the bereaved individual's self-esteem is generally preserved. He or she may think about death or dying, but those thoughts are focused on joining the deceased (APA, 2013).

*Grief:* An intense set of emotional reactions in response to a real, imagined, or anticipated loss. Real grief occurs in relation to a recognizable event, existing or happening as a fact. Examples: death, car accident, tragedy. Imagined grief is a picture, pretense, assumption or fantasy of what might have been.

Example: the normal potential of a physically or mentally deformed child, the monetary investment payoff, the promised but undelivered career promotion. Anticipated grief is based on looking ahead, predicting, expecting or preparing oneself for an impending loss. Examples: terminal illness, divorce, loved ones who are missing in action (Schupp, 2003).

*Prolonged grief disorder:*   A disorder described by Prigerson, et al. (2007) that was proposed, but not included, in the DSM-5. Nevertheless, it deserves our consideration and attention, because it may accompany trauma. It is a severe psychological wounding caused by a significant loss. The symptoms must be marked and persistent for 6 months before the diagnosis can be made. This grief exceeds the realm of normalcy, and, using Prigerson's criteria, would be classified as a mental disorder (Prigerson, 2007).

*Major depressive disorder:*   Characterized by discrete episodes of at least 2 weeks' duration. It involves clear-cut changes in affect, cognition, and neurovegetative functions with inter-episodic remissions. Major depressive disorder is the classic or "common cold" of the depressive disorders. At least one of the symptoms is either a depressed mood or a loss of interest or pleasure nearly every day (APA, 2013).

*Persistent depressive disorder (dysthymia):*   A consolidation of DSM-IV defined chronic major depressive disorder and dysthymic disorder. Dsythymia has not been eliminated, but has been included as part of a new diagnosis. The individual must experience a depressed mood for at least two years. Criteria for major depressive disorder must be continuously present for those two years. They must have two or more of the following: poor appetite or overeating, insomnia or hypersomnia, low energy or fatigue, low self-esteem, poor concentration or difficulty making decisions or feelings of hopelessness. This diagnosis will probably be given to a limited number of individuals (APA, 2013).

*Dissociative identity disorder (DID):*   The presence of two or more distinct personality states or an experience of being possessed. The disruption is so extreme that there will be sustained periods of identity disruption when psychosocial pressures are severe or prolonged. This disorder was originally referred to as multiple personality disorder (APA, 2013).

**Dissociation:**   The splitting off of clusters of mental contents from conscious awareness which is central to dissociative disorders. The term is also used to describe the separation of an idea from its emotional significance and affect, as seen in the inappropriate affect in schizophrenia. Often a result of psychic trauma, dissociation may allow the individual to maintain allegiance to two contradictory truths while remaining unconscious of the contradiction. An extreme manifestation of dissociation is dissociative identity disorder, in which a person may exhibit several independent personalities, each unaware of the others (APA, 2013).

**Brief psychotic disorder:**   A disturbance which involves the sudden onset of at least one psychotic symptom such as delusions, hallucinations, disorganized speech, and abnormal psychomotor behavior. The duration of the disturbance is at least one day but less than 1 month with the person eventually returning to their normal level of functioning (APA, 2013).

**Depersonalization:**   The experience of feeling detached from, and as if one is an outside observer of, one's mental processes, body, or actions (e.g., feeling like one is in a dream; a sense of unreality of self, perceptual alterations; emotional and/or physical numbing; temporal distortions; sense of unreality). Derealization/depersonalization have been combined in DSM-5 and are classified together as derealization/depersonalization (APA, 2013).

**Obsessive-compulsive disorder:**   Characterized by the presence of obsessions and/or compulsions. Obsessions are recurrent and persistent thoughts, urges, or images that are experienced as intrusive and unwanted, whereas compulsions are repetitive behaviors or mental acts that an individual feels driven to perform in response to an obsession or according to rules that must be applied rigidly. Others in the category of obsessive-compulsive and related disorders are also characterized by preoccupations and by repetitive behaviors or mental acts in response to the preoccupations (APA, 2013).

**Borderline personality disorder:**   Typical features such as instability of self-image, personal goals, interpersonal relationships, and affects accompanied by impulsivity, risk taking, and/or hostility. Difficulties are apparent in identity, self-direction, empathy, and/or intimacy, along with specific maladaptive traits in the domain of negative affectivity, and also antagonism and/or disinhibition (APA, 2013).

**Substance use disorders:** A cluster of cognitive, behavioral, and physiological symptoms indicating that the individual continues using the substance despite significant substance-related problems (APA, 2013).

**Somatic symptom disorder:** Disorder typified by multiple, current, somatic symptoms that are distressing or result in significant disruption of daily life, although sometimes only one severe symptom, most commonly pain, is present. Symptoms may be specific (e.g., localized pain) or relatively nonspecific (e.g., fatigue). The symptoms sometimes represent normal bodily sensations or discomfort that does not generally signify serious disease. Somatic symptoms without an evident medical explanation are not sufficient to make this diagnosis. The individual's suffering is authentic, whether or not it is medically explained. An individual must also have excessive thoughts, feelings or behaviors that are related to the somatic symptoms. They must have one of the following: 1. persistent thoughts that are disproportionate about the seriousness of their symptoms, and, 2. a persistently high level of anxiety about symptoms, or 3. excessive time and energy devoted to the symptoms. Although any one somatic symptom may not be continuously present, the state of being symptomatic is persistent (typically more than 6 months). (APA, 2013).

**Eating disorders:** Disorders characterized by a persistent disturbance of eating or eating-related behavior that results in the altered consumption or absorption of food and that significantly impairs physical health or psychosocial functioning. Diagnostic criteria are provided for pica, rumination disorder, avoidant/restrictive food intake disorder, anorexia nervosa, bulimia nervosa, and binge-eating disorder (APA, 2013).

**Derealization:** The experience of feeling detached from, as if one is an outside observer of, one's surroundings (e.g., individuals or objects are experienced as unreal, dreamlike, foggy, lifeless, or visually distorted). Derealization/depersonalization have been combined in DSM-5 and are classified together as derealization/depersonalization (APA, 2013).

## RELEVANT CHANGES FROM DSM-IV-TR TO DSM-5

*TRAUMA- AND STRESSOR-RELATED DISORDERS* is now a new chapter in DSM-5.

***PTSD*** (posttraumatic stress disorder) (309.81) has three major changes:

1. The criterion for the subjective response to traumatic events, i.e. experiencing 'fear, helplessness, or horror' has been eliminated in DSM-5.

2. The criterion for stressors to qualify as traumatic experiences has changed from three symptom clusters in DSM-IV-TR (re-experiencing, avoidance/numbing, and arousal) to four symptom clusters in DSM-5; this is because the avoidance/numbing cluster has been divided into two separate clusters: avoidance and persistent negative alterations in cognitions and mood. The numbing cluster retains most of DSM-IV-TR criteria and adds persistent negative emotional states.

3. Separate criteria have been added for children 6 years old and younger and diagnostic thresholds have been lowered for children and adolescents.

***ACUTE STRESS DISORDER*** (308.3) has three major changes:

1. It is more specific about whether trauma is experienced directly, witnessed, or experienced indirectly;

2. It eliminates the criteria for experiencing "fear, helplessness, or horror."

3. The DSM-IV-TR listed five types of dissociation, and an individual needed to have three to fulfill the criteria. In the DSM-5, dissociation is listed as one out of five categories that a person can experience. It uses the two following dissociative symptoms:

   (a) derealization—an altered sense of the reality of one's surroundings or oneself (e.g., seeing oneself from another's perspective, being in a daze, time slowing), and

   (b) the inability to remember an important aspect of the traumatic event(s) (typically due to dissociative amnesia and not to other factors such as head injury, alcohol, or drugs).

***ADJUSTMENT DISORDERS*** has two major changes:

1. Adjustment disorders have changed from a residual category in DSM-IV-TR to a continuum of stress responses to traumatic and non-traumatic events.

2. The two subtypes of reactive attachment disorder in DSM-IV-TR have changed into two separate disorders in DSM-5: Reactive attachment disorder (313.89) and disinhibited social engagement disorder (313.89).

**DISSOCIATIVE DISORDERS** (300.14) have three major changes:

1. DID (Dissociative identity disorder): criteria now state that symptoms of identity disruption may be reported as well as observed, and gaps in recall of events may occur for everyday events, not just for traumatic events.
2. Derealization is now included in depersonalization disorder, which in DSM-5 is called depersonalization/derealization disorder.
3. Dissociative fugue is a specifier of dissociative amnesia in DSM-5, not a separate disorder as in DSM-IV-TR.

**DEPRESSIVE DISORDERS** have four major changes:

1. Dysthymia in DSVIV-TR is now titled persistent depressive disorder (300.4) in DSM-5. It combines chronic major depressive disorder and dysthymic disorder.
2. Disruptive mood dysregulation disorder (296.99) is a new diagnosis in DSM-5. It is used for children up to age 18 with irritability and frequent extreme behavioral episodes; the goal is to prevent over-diagnosis of bipolar disorders in children.
3. Premenstrual dysphoric disorder (625.4) is now listed as a primary depressive disorder in DSM-5, not in appendix B as in DSM-IV-TR
4. DSM-5 eliminates the bereavement exclusion of depressive symptoms lasting less than 2 months following the death of loved one. DSM-5 recognizes that depressive symptoms of bereavement can last 12 years or more.

**ANXIETY DISORDERS** have five major changes:

1. DSM-5 no longer lists OCD, PTSD, & acute stress disorder under anxiety disorders.
2. Specific phobia and social anxiety disorder (social phobia) (300.23) diagnoses no longer require criteria of excessive or unreasonable anxiety for persons over age 18.
3. In DSM-5, panic disorder (300.01) and agoraphobia (300.02) are two separate diagnoses, no longer linked as in DSM-IV-TR, i.e. panic disorder with or without agoraphobia.
4. In DSM-5, panic attacks are listed as a specifier applicable to all DSM-5 disorders.
5. Separation anxiety disorder (309.21) and selective mutism (312.23) are added to the anxiety disorder classification in DSM-5.

**OBSESSIVE-COMPULSIVE AND RELATED DISORDERS (300.3):** This is a new chapter in DSM-5. New disorders in this chapter include:

- Hoarding disorder (300.3)
- Excoriation (skin picking) disorder (698.4)
- Substance/medication induced obsessive-compulsive and related disorders (ICD-9-CM and ICD-10-CM)
- Obsessive compulsive & related disorder due to another medical condition (294.8)
- Trichotillomania (hair pulling disorders) (312.39) has moved from DSM-IV-TR classification in impulse control disorders NOS to this chapter of obsessive-compulsive and related disorders in DSM-5.
- Body dysmorphic disorder, (300.7) in DSM-5 has added the specifier "muscle dysmorphia."
- Other categories in this chapter include other specified obsessive-compulsive and related disorders (300.3) and unspecified obsessive-compulsive and related disorders (300.3).

## THE TRAUMA MEMBRANE

There is much debate in the field of traumatology regarding early interventions. In physiological trauma we know that a quick intervention is often needed to save a life, and minutes can make a difference between life or death outcomes. Very rarely would an early intervention cause difficulty in such emergency situations; however, psychological trauma operates within a different set of rules. Early therapeutic interventions could re-traumatize a victim if pursued prior to the stabilization of the client. The Hippocratic Oath *"do no harm"* applies to both the physiological and psychological arenas. Lindy (1996) reminds clinicians that with some trauma, it is a normal adaptation for survivors to use denial and forgetting. They are simply buying time by setting the issue aside. It will be dealt with in small doses as the client is able to bear it. Raphael and Wilson (2000) believe that these emergency defenses may be correlated with the helpful release of neuro-hormones.

If clients are viewed as resistant or in denial, issues whose discussion should be delayed may be forced to the surface and could cause damage. Lindy and Wilson (2001) explain that the metaphorical *"trauma membrane"* protects the person from an overload of remembering. It is defined as *"the sealing off of traumatic experiences as an adaptive process in the initial phase."* Sigmund Freud

(1955/1920) was an early spokesperson regarding the severity of trauma and its effect. He explained that: *"Trauma by definition overwhelms the protective barrier of defenses; it disrupts the stimulus barrier."* Lindy and Wilson (2001) add that, *"it tears a hole in the survivors' belief that they can handle whatever befalls them."*

Horowitz (1999) reminds us that *"talking"* can be helpful right after a disaster, because it promotes understanding and reduces irrational fantasies about why the tragedy occurred. However, each person has a coping style and they don't all process in the same manner. Horowitz (1999) explains: "Some people seek out every bit of information; others need time for 'dosing' to take in one tolerable bit of meaning at a time, and still others need to take some time off for recovery."

Children in particular may handle trauma in bits and pieces. They may talk about it for a few minutes and then run and play. It should not be interpreted as *"not caring."* It is simply a child's way of handling it.

Survivors with trauma-related conditions may make valiant attempts to avoid any reminders of the horror they experienced. This theoretical trauma membrane assists with their endeavors of avoidance. Lindy (1985) defines and states the purpose of this trauma membrane. It is a, "semi-permeable membrane which covers the space left in the repression barrier by the trauma experiences. It is designed to keep trauma reminding stimuli out and to let in only stimuli that will soothe the wound." Clinicians would do well to respect these natural protective defenses and work in harmony with them, rather than disrupt them. We must bide our time and wait until the traumatized client is stabilized and invites us to walk behind the membrane with them.

## THE TRAUMA INTAKE INTERVIEW

Most assessment and diagnosis of a client occurs during the initial intake interview. Hospitals, clinics, agencies, or organizations generally have their own standard intake interviews that evaluate psychological disturbance.

John Briere (1997) explains that in the interview session, the client is typically evaluated for:

- altered mental status (i.e., for evidence of dementia, confusion, disorientation, delirium, retardation, or other cognitive-organic disturbance);
- psychotic symptoms (e.g., hallucinations, delusions, formal thought disorder, negative signs);
- evidence of self-injurious or suicidal thoughts and behaviors;

- potential danger to others;
- mood disturbance (i.e., depression, anxiety);
- substance abuse or addiction; and
- personality dysfunction.

In combination with other information (e.g., from the client, significant others, and outside agencies), these interview data provide the basis for diagnosis and an intervention plan.

Although the previous elements are essential for accurate diagnosis, they may not be all-inclusive. Briere (1997) provides clinicians with a timely warning:

> If the presenting problem is a posttraumatic reaction, these standard clinical screens may miss important information. When there is a possibility of trauma-related disturbance, the interview should consider investigating the following additional components, if time allows and the client is sufficiently stable.

**Symptoms of Posttraumatic Stress**

- Intrusive symptoms such as flashbacks, nightmares, intrusive thoughts and memories, reliving experiences, distress or physiological reaction to trauma-reminiscent cues
- Avoidant symptoms such as behavioral or cognitive attempts to avoid trauma-reminiscent stimuli, or psychic numbing
- Hyper arousal symptoms such as decreased or restless sleep, muscle tension, irritability, jumpiness, or attention-concentration difficulties

**Dissociative responses**

- Depersonalization or derealization
- Fugue states
- 'Spacing out' or cognitive disengagement
- Trance states
- Amnesia or missing time
- Identity alteration

## Somatic disturbance

- Conversion reactions (e.g., paralysis, anesthesia, blindness, deafness)
- Somatization
- Psychogenic pain (e.g., pelvic pain, chronic pain)

## Sexual disturbance

- Sexual distress (including sexual dysfunction)
- Sexual fears and conflicts

## Trauma-related cognitive disturbance

- Low self-esteem
- Helplessness
- Hopelessness
- Overvalued ideas regarding the level of danger in the environment
- Idealization of perpetrators

## Tension-reduction activities (Briere, 1996)

- Self-mutilation
- Bingeing-purging
- Dysfunctional sexual behavior (including sex 'addiction')
- Compulsive stealing
- Impulsive violent behavior

## Transient posttraumatic psychotic reactions

- Stress-induced cognitive slippage, loosened associations
- Stress-induced hallucinations (often trauma congruent)
- Stress-induced delusions (often trauma congruent, especially paranoia)

In addition to these areas, no assessment is complete without evaluating the impact of losses in life and their accompanying grief. The following list may be useful in the interview process to ensure that adequate attention has been given to grief-related concerns.

## Loss/Grief Inventory
### Common Factors That Complicate Grief and Trauma Resolution

### Emotional

- Unexpressed hostility
- Prolonged duration of grief
- Delayed and insufficient responses
- Excessive and disabling reactions
- Repressed emotions or absence of emotion
- Unresolved previous losses
- Concomitant losses

### Relational

- Narcissistic relationship
- Overly dependent relationship
- Child abuse or childhood trauma
- Insecure childhood attachments
- Death of a child
- Ambivalent relationship with deceased
- Death following a lingering illness
- Uncertain death or missing in action (MIA)
- Holding onto false hopes
- Sudden unexpected death or loss

### Personal

- Self-blame for abuse issues
- History of depressive illness
- Personality factors
- Self-concept roles
- Belief that loss was avoidable
- Social problems

# THE LOSS/TRAUMA HISTORY

All routine intake interviews should include a loss/trauma history. Bessel van der Kolk (1996) stated clearly that many clients have multiple traumas and losses and do not present with classic PTSD symptoms. All loss and trauma throughout life must be evaluated as to its current impact on the client's presenting problem.

Please state age of person when trauma occurred on the top line.

Briefly describe trauma on line below. Use as many lines as needed.

Example:

| 4 years of age | 16 years of age | 45 years of age | 65 years of age |
|---|---|---|---|
| Mother committed suicide | Lost leg in car accident | Went through divorce | Had colon cancer |
| | | | |
| | | | |
| | | | |
| | | | |
| | | | |
| | | | |

## THE INTER-RELATEDNESS OF GRIEF, DEPRESSION AND TRAUMA

Although the focus of this publication resides in the field of traumatology, we cannot overlook the inter-relatedness between grief and trauma. It behooves clinicians to reconsider the artificial boundary lines between what has traditionally been viewed as two distinct fields of traumatology and grief. The two fields are more intimately related than originally believed. Bereavement professionals, thanatologists, and traumatologists use the word *"grief"* to describe either an emotion or a process. The use of grief in either fashion connects it to a loss. A few definitions are worthy of consideration. Some early definitions are still true to the field of grief.

> *"Intense emotional suffering caused by loss, disaster, etc., acute sorrow, deep sadness."*
>
> Webster's New World Dictionary, 1970

> *"An intense emotional state associated with the loss of someone (or something) with whom (or which) one has had a deep bond. Not used as a synonym for depression."*
>
> Arthur S. Reber
> The Penguin Dictionary of Psychology, 1995

> *"Grief is an intense set of emotional reactions in response to a real, imagined, or anticipated loss."*
>
> Linda J. Schupp
> Grief: Normal, Complicated, Traumatic, 2003

Loss is the prerequisite for grief and the entrance into its domain. When we view grief as real, imagined, or anticipated losses, then its pervasiveness and impact is clearly seen.

**Real**—a recognizable event, existing or happening as a fact. Example: death, car accident, tragedy.

**Imagined**—a picture, pretense, assumption, or fantasy of what might have been. Example: the normal potential of a physically or mentally handicapped child, the monetary investment payoff, the promised but undelivered career promotion.

**Anticipated**—looking ahead, predicting, expecting, or preparing oneself for an impending loss. Example: terminal illness, divorce, loved ones who are missing in action.

Linda J. Schupp
*Grief: Normal, Complicated, Traumatic*, 2003

Although most research and clinical interventions have focused on the loss of a loved one, the significance and importance of any type of real, imagined, or anticipated loss is person specific and all-encompassing.

| Common Losses | | |
|---|---|---|
| Loved Ones | Animal companions | Dreams |
| Marriage | Amputation of body part | Meaning in life |
| Career | Potential of self or others | Confidence |
| Home | Image | Faith |
| Health | Safety | Love |
| Appearance | Security | Dignity |
| Mobility | Finances | Identity |
| Status | Material Possessions | Lifestyle |

Given this foundation of loss as the etiology of grief, we can conclude that:

*A person may experience grief without trauma, but not trauma without grief.*

Early researchers in the study of grief and trauma such as Erich Lindemann and Alexandra Adler, who worked with survivors of the Coconut Grove fire in Boston, Massachusetts, can provide us with some observations regarding the interrelatedness of grief and trauma. Lindemann (1944) counseled, studied, and wrote about the normal and abnormal grief reactions of the survivors of the fire while working at the Massachusetts General Hospital. The subject and impact of grief had been given very little recognition until Lindemann published his study in 1944, *Symptomatology and Management of Acute Grief*. His work paved the way for further studies on the effects of grief. Adler (1943) also worked with bereaved survivors in the emergency room of the Boston

City Hospital just across town from Lindemann. She appears to be the first individual to write about the effects of trauma on grieving. In her opinion, it wasn't just the death and loss of a loved one that caused distress, but the horrific circumstances of the death must also be considered.

Therese Rando (1993), a respected researcher and later contributor in both grief and trauma, indicates that there are six primary factors which contribute to a traumatic death:

1. Suddenness and lack of anticipation
2. Violence, mutilation, and destruction
3. Preventability and/or randomness
4. Loss of a child
5. Multiple deaths
6. Survivors of a personal encounter with death secondary to either a significant threat to survival or a massive and/or shocking configuration with the death and mutilation of others.

Adler (1943) viewed the trauma itself as the most difficult aspect of the loss. Her paper, *Neuropsychiatric complications in victims of Boston's Coconut Grove disaster* began the research on traumatic distress. Even today, grief hasn't been fully identified as the traumatic stressor that it truly is, but concepts are changing, and grief is increasingly being elevated in importance.

From those roots, many studies have come forth, culminating in the inclusion of a diagnosis of posttraumatic stress disorder in the DSM-III in 1980. Finally, a trauma-related disorder had been officially recognized and accepted as a legitimate diagnosis.

Grief at this time is excluded from significant diagnoses in the DSM-IV-TR and the DSM-5 and hasn't received a mental disorder recognition. Prigerson et.al. (2007) attempted to have her prolonged grief disorder become a part of the DSM-5. However, it was not accepted, and it appears that the true impact of severe grief is still not recognized. Many clinicians will continue to use Holly Prigerson's prolonged grief disorder and, hopefully, its importance will be acknowledged.

Trauma issues must be dealt with first prior to grief counseling. The client must be stabilized before beginning to evaluate the enormity of the loss, otherwise the psyche may be overwhelmed and the person re-traumatized. Clinicians must respect the *"trauma membrane"* in these cases and handle elements as the client is able to bear it.

We certainly must include depression as part of the trauma experience. It behooves us to look at the DSM-5 for major depressive disorder (MDD). We also need to distinguish MDD from normal grief. They can appear similar, but the criteria for major depressive disorder distinguish between depression and grief.

## Major Depressive Disorder DSM-5

### Diagnostic Criteria

**A.** Five (or more) of the following symptoms have been present during the same 2-week period and represent a change from previous functioning; at least one of the symptoms is either (1) depressed mood or (2) loss of interest or pleasure.

**Note:** Do not include symptoms that are clearly attributable to another medical condition.

1. Depressed mood most of the day, nearly every day, as indicated by either subjective report (e.g., feels sad, empty, hopeless) or observation made by others (e.g., appears tearful). (**Note:** In children and adolescents, can be irritable mood.)

2. Markedly diminished interest or pleasure in all, or almost all, activities most of the day, nearly every day (as indicated by either subjective account or observation).

3. Significant weight loss when not dieting or weight gain (e.g., a change of more than 5% of body weight in a month), or decrease or increase in appetite nearly every day. (**Note:** In children, consider failure to make expected weight gain.)

4. Insomnia or hypersomnia nearly every day.

5. Psychomotor agitation or retardation nearly every day (observable by others, not merely subjective feelings of restlessness or being slowed down).

6. Fatigue or loss of energy nearly every day.

7. Feelings of worthlessness or excessive or inappropriate guilt (which may be delusional) nearly every day (not merely self-reproach or guilt about being sick).

8. Diminished ability to think or concentrate, or indecisiveness, nearly every day (either by subjective account or as observed by others).

9. Recurrent thoughts of death (not just fear of dying), recurrent suicidal ideation without a specific plan, or a suicide attempt or a specific plan for committing suicide.

**B.** The symptoms cause clinically significant distress or impairment in social, occupational, or other important areas of functioning.

**C.** The episode is not attributable to the physiological effects of a substance or to another medical condition.

**Note:** Criterion A-C represents a major depressive episode.

**Note:** Responses to a significant loss (e.g. bereavement, financial ruin, losses from a natural disaster, a serious medical illness or disability) may include the feelings of intense sadness, rumination about the loss, insomnia, poor appetite, and weight loss noted in Criterion A, which may resemble a depressive episode. Although such symptoms may be understandable or considered appropriate to the loss, the presence of a major depressive episode in addition to the normal response to a significant loss should also be carefully considered. This decision inevitably requires the exercise of clinical judgment based on the individual's history and the cultural norms for the expression of distress in the context of loss.

**D.** The occurrence of the major depressive episode is not better explained by schizoaffective disorder, schizophrenia, schizophreniform disorder, delusional disorder, or other specified and unspecified schizophrenia spectrum and other psychotic disorders.

**E.** There has never been a manic episode or a hypomanic episode.

**Note:** This exclusion does not apply if all of the manic-like or hypomanic-like episodes are substance-induced or are attributable to the physiological effects of another medical condition.

In distinguishing grief from a major depressive episode (MDE), it is useful to consider that in grief the predominant affect is feelings of emptiness and loss, while in MDE it is persistent depressed mood and the inability to anticipate happiness or pleasure. The dysphoria in grief is likely to decrease in intensity over days to weeks and occurs in waves, the so-called pangs of grief. These waves tend to be associated with thoughts or reminders of the deceased. The depressed mood of MDE is more persistent and not tied to specific thoughts or preoccupations. The pain of grief may be accompanied by positive emotions and humor that are uncharacteristic of the pervasive unhappiness and misery characteristic of MDE. The thought content associated with grief generally features a preoccupation with thoughts and memories of the deceased, rather than the self-critical or pessimistic ruminations seen in

MDE. In grief, self-esteem is generally preserved, whereas in MDE feelings of worthlessness and self-loathing are common. If self-derogatory ideation is present in grief, it typically involves perceived failings vis-á-vis the deceased (e.g., not visiting frequently enough, not telling the deceased how much he or she was loved). If a bereaved individual thinks about death and dying, such thoughts are generally focused on the deceased and possibly about "joining" the deceased, whereas in MDE such thoughts are focused on ending one's own life because of feeling worthless, undeserving of life, or unable to cope with the pain of depression.

### Coding and Recording Procedures

The diagnostic code for major depressive disorder is based on whether this is a single or recurrent episode, current severity, presence of psychotic features, and remission status. Current severity and psychotic features are only indicated if full criteria are currently met for a major depressive episode. Remission specifiers are only indicated if the full criteria are not currently met for a major depressive episode. Codes are as follows:

In recording a diagnosis, terms should be listed in the following order: major depressive disorder, single or recurrent episode, severity/psychotic/remission specifiers, followed by as many of the following specifiers without codes that apply to the current episode.

| Severity/course specifier | Single episode | Recurrent episode |
|---|---|---|
| Mild (p. 188) | 296.21 (F32.0) | 296.31 (F33.0) |
| Moderate (p. 188) | 296.22 (F32.1) | 296.32 (F33.1) |
| Severe (p. 188) | 296.23 (F32.2) | 296.33 (F33.2) |
| With psychotic features** (p. 186) | 296.24 (F32.3) | 296.34 (F33.3) |
| In partial remission (p. 188) | 296.25 (F32.4) | 296.35 (F33.41) |
| In full remission (p. 188) | 296.26 (F32.5) | 296.36 (F33.42) |
| Unspecified | 296.20 (F32.9) | 296.30 (F33.9) |

\* For an episode to be considered recurrent there must be an interval of at least 2 consecutive months between separate episodes in which criteria are not met for a major depressive episode. The definitions of specifiers are found on the indicated pages.

\*\* If psychotic features are present, code the "with psychotic features" specifier irrespective of episode severity.

Specify:

**With anxious distress**

**With mixed features**

**With melancholic features**

**With atypical features**

**With mood-congruent psychotic features**

**With mood-incongruent psychotic features**

**With catatonia** *Coding note: Use additional code 293.89*

**With peripartum onset**

**With seasonal pattern** (recurrent episode only)

It is important to reiterate and remind ourselves that grief occurs with any significant loss. The DSM-5 focuses only on the loss of a person, but grief encompasses any major loss in life.

## Persistent Depressive Disorder (Dysthymia) DSM-5

### Diagnostic Criteria

Persistent depressive disorder 300.4 (F34.1) represents a consolidation of DSM-IV-TR defined chronic major depressive disorder and dysthymic disorder.

**A.** Depressed mood for most of the day, for more days than not, as indicated by either subjective account or observation by others, for at least 2 years.

**Note:** In children and adolescents, mood can be irritable and duration must be at least 1 year.

**B.** Presence, while depressed, of two (or more) of the following:

**1.** Poor appetite or overeating.

**2.** Insomnia or hypersomnia.

**3.** Low energy or fatigue.

**4.** Low self-esteem.

**5.** Poor concentration or difficulty making decisions.

**6.** Feelings of hopelessness.

**C.** During the 2-year period (1 year for children or adolescents) of the disturbance, the individual has never been without the symptoms in Criteria A and B for more than 2 months at a time.

**D.** Criteria for a major depressive disorder may be continuously present for 2 years.

**E.** There has never been a manic episode or a hypomanic episode, and criteria have never been met for cyclothymic disorder.

**F.** The disturbance is not better explained by persistent schizoaffective disorder, schizophrenia, delusional disorder, or other specified or unspecified schizophrenia spectrum and other psychotic disorder.

**G.** The symptoms are not attributable to the physiological effects of a substance (e.g., a drug of abuse, a medication) or another medical condition (e.g. hypothyroidism).

**H.** The symptoms cause clinically significant distress or impairment in social, occupational, or other important areas of functioning.

**Note:** Because the criteria for a major depressive episode include four symptoms that are absent from the symptom list for persistent depressive disorder (dysthymia), a very limited number of individuals will have depressive symptoms that have persisted longer than 2 years but will not meet criteria for persistent depressive disorder. If full criteria for a major depressive episode have been met at some point during the current episode of illness, they should be given a diagnosis of major depressive disorder. Otherwise, a diagnosis of other specified depressive disorder or unspecified depressive disorder is warranted.

*Specify* if:

**With anxious distress**

**With mixed features**

**With melancholic features**

**With atypical features**

**With mood-congruent psychotic features**

**With mood-incongruent psychotic features**

**With peripartum onset**

*Specify* if:

**In partial remission**
**In full remission**

*Specify* if:

**Early onset:** If onset is before age 21 years.

**Late onset:** If onset is at age 21 years or older.

*Specify* if: (for most recent 2 years of persistent depressive disorder):

**With pure dysthymic syndrome:** Full criteria for a major depressive episode have not been met in at least the preceding 2 years.

**With persistent major depressive episode:** Full criteria for a major depressive episode have been met throughout the preceding 2-year period.

**With intermittent major depressive episodes, with current episode:** Full criteria for a major depressive episode are currently met, but there have been periods of at least 8 weeks in at least the preceding 2 years with symptoms below the threshold for a full major depressive episode.

**With intermittent major depressive episodes, without current episode:** Full criteria for a major depressive episode are not currently met, but there have been one or more major depressive episodes in at least the preceding 2 years.

*Specify* current severity:

**Mild**

**Moderate**

**Severe**

Severity is based on the number of criterion symptoms, the severity of those symptoms, and the degree of functional disability.

**Mild:** Few, if any, symptoms in excess of those required to make the diagnosis are present, the intensity of the symptoms is distressing but manageable, and the symptoms result in minor impairment in social or occupational functioning.

**Moderate:** The numbers of symptoms, intensity of symptoms, and/or functional impairment are between those specified for "mild" and "severe."

**Severe:** The number of symptoms is substantially in excess of that required to make the diagnosis, the intensity of the symptoms is seriously distressing and unmanageable, and the symptoms markedly interfere with social and occupational functioning.

## Five Significant Trauma-Related Criteria

There are four criteria for diagnosing PTSD or related symptoms and one criterion for grief.

1. Posttraumatic stress disorder (APA, 2013)
2. Acute stress disorder (APA, 2013)
3. Prolonged grief disorder (Prigerson, et al., 2007)
4. Complex Posttraumatic Stress Disorder (Herman, 1992)
5. Developmental Trauma Disorder (van der Kolk, 2005)

It is relatively easy to diagnose PTSD and ASD with the DSM-5 stated criteria. Although complex PTSD and prolonged grief disorder did not become part of DSM-5, they definitely deserve our attention. The DSM-5 criteria fall short in capturing all the elements of PTSD. Herman's (1992) complex PTSD is commonly used and accepted particularly for clients with repeated prolonged abuse. The consensus criteria for prolonged grief disorder (Prigerson, et al., 2007) have been receiving recognition and are being used as well. Clinicians need to familiarize themselves with these five criteria for a more thorough and accurate diagnosis.

## Posttraumatic Stress Disorder DSM-IV-TR

### *Diagnostic Criteria*

A. The person has been exposed to a traumatic event in which both of the following were present:
   1. The person experienced, witnessed, or was confronted with an event or events that involved actual or threatened death or serious injury, or a threat to the physical integrity of self or others.

**2.** The person's response involved intense fear, helplessness, or horror. **Note:** In children, this may be expressed instead by disorganized or agitated behavior.

**B.** The traumatic event is persistently re-experienced in one (or more) of the following ways:

**1.** Recurrent and intrusive distressing recollections of the event, including images, thoughts, or perceptions. **Note:** In young children, repetitive play may occur in which themes or aspects of the trauma are expressed.

**2.** Recurrent distressing dreams of the event. **Note:** In children, there may be frightening dreams without recognizable content.

**3.** Acting or feeling as if the traumatic event were recurring (includes a sense of reliving the experience, illusions, hallucinations, and dissociative flashback episodes, including those that occur on awakening or when intoxicated). **Note:** In young children, trauma-specific re-enactment may occur.

**4.** Intense psychological distress at exposure to internal or external cues that symbolize or resemble an aspect of the traumatic event.

**5.** Physiological reactivity on exposure to internal or external cues that symbolize or resemble an aspect of the traumatic event.

**C.** Persistent avoidance of stimuli associated with the trauma and numbing of general responsiveness (not present before the trauma), as indicated by three (or more) of the following:

**1.** Efforts to avoid thoughts, feelings, or conversations associated with the trauma

**2.** Efforts to avoid activities, places, or people that arouse recollections of the trauma

**3.** Inability to recall an important aspect of the trauma

**4.** Markedly diminished interest or participation in significant activities

**5.** Feeling of detachment or estrangement from others

**6.** Restricted range of affect (e.g., unable to have loving feelings)

**7.** Sense of foreshortened future (e.g., does not expect to have a career, marriage, children, or a normal life span)

    **D.** Persistent symptoms of increased arousal (not present before the trauma), as indicated by two (or more) of the following:

        **1.** Difficulty falling or staying asleep

        **2.** Irritability or outbursts of anger

        **3.** Difficulty concentrating

        **4.** Hyper vigilance

        **5.** exaggerated startle response

    **E.** Duration of the disturbance (symptoms in criteria B, C, and D) is longer than one month.

    **F.** The disturbance causes clinically significant distress or impairment in social, occupational, or other important areas of functioning.

*Specify if:*

    **Acute:** if duration of symptoms is less than 3 months.

    **Chronic:** if duration of symptoms is 3 months or more.

*Specify if:*

    **With Delayed Onset:** if onset of symptoms is at least 6 months after the stressor (APA, 2000).

## POSTTRAUMATIC STRESS DISORDER DSM-5 DIAGNOSTIC CRITERIA: 309.81 (F43.10)

### Posttraumatic Stress Disorder

**Note:** The following criteria apply to adults, adolescents, and children older than 6 years. For children 6 years and younger, see corresponding criteria below.

    **A.** Exposure to actual or threatened death, serious injury, or sexual violence in one (or more) of the following ways:

        **1.** Directly experiencing the traumatic event(s).

        **2.** Witnessing, in person, the event(s) as it occurred to others.

        **3.** Learning that the traumatic event(s) occurred to a close family member or close friend. In cases of actual or threatened death of a family member or friend, the event(s) must have been violent or accidental.

**4.** Experiencing repeated or extreme exposure to aversive details of the traumatic event(s) (e.g., first responders collecting human remains; police officers repeatedly exposed to details of child abuse).

**Note:** Criterion A does not apply to exposure through electronic media, television, movies, or pictures, unless this exposure is work-related.

**B.** Presence of one (or more) of the following intrusion symptoms associated with the traumatic event(s), beginning after the traumatic event(s) occurred:

**1.** Recurrent, involuntary, and intrusive distressing memories of the traumatic event(s).

**Note:** In children older than 6 years, repetitive play may occur in which themes or aspects of the traumatic event(s) are expressed.

**2.** Recurrent distressing dreams in which the content and/or affect of the dream are related to the traumatic event(s).

**Note:** In children, there may be frightening dreams without recognizable content.

**3.** Dissociative reactions (e.g., flashbacks) in which the individual feels or acts as if the traumatic event(s) were recurring. (Such reactions may occur on a continuum, with the most extreme expression being a complete loss of awareness of present surroundings.)

**Note:** In children, trauma-specific reenactment may occur in play.

**4.** Intense or prolonged psychological distress at exposure to internal or external cues that symbolize or resemble an aspect of the traumatic event(s).

**5.** Marked physiological reactions to internal or external cues that symbolize or resemble an aspect of the traumatic event(s).

**C.** Persistent avoidance of stimuli associated with the traumatic event(s), beginning after the traumatic event(s) occurred, as evidenced by one or both of the following:

**1.** Avoidance of, or efforts to avoid, distressing memories, thoughts, or feelings about, or closely associated with, the traumatic event(s).

**2.** Avoidance of, or efforts to avoid, external reminders (people, places, conversations, activities, objects, situations) that arouse distressing memories, thoughts, or feelings about or closely associated with the traumatic event(s).

**D.** Negative alterations in cognitions and mood associated with the traumatic event(s), beginning or worsening after the traumatic event(s) occurred, as evidenced by two (or more) of the following:

   **1.** Inability to remember an important aspect of the traumatic event(s) (typically due to dissociative amnesia and not to other factors such as head injury, alcohol, or drugs).

   **2.** Persistent and exaggerated negative beliefs or expectations about oneself, others, or the world (e.g., "I am bad," "No one can be trusted," "The world is completely dangerous," "My whole nervous system is permanently ruined").

   **3.** Persistent, distorted cognitions about the cause or consequences of the traumatic event(s) that lead the individual to blame himself/herself or others.

   **4.** Persistent negative emotional state (e.g., fear, horror, anger, guilt, or shame).

   **5.** Markedly diminished interest or participation in significant activities.

   **6.** Feelings of detachment or estrangement from others.

   **7.** Persistent inability to experience positive emotions (e.g., inability to experience happiness, satisfaction, or loving feelings).

**E.** Marked alterations in arousal and reactivity associated with the traumatic event(s), beginning or worsening after the traumatic event(s) occurred, as evidenced by two (or more) of the following:

   **1.** Irritable behavior and angry outbursts (with little or no provocation) typically expressed as verbal or physical aggression toward people or objects.

   **2.** Reckless or self-destructive behavior.

   **3.** Hyper vigilance.

   **4.** Exaggerated startle response.

   **5.** Problems with concentration.

   **6.** Sleep disturbance (e.g., difficulty falling or staying asleep or restless sleep).

**F.** Duration of the disturbance (Criteria B, C, D, and E) is more than 1 month.

**G.** The disturbance causes clinically significant distress or impairment in social, occupational, or other important areas of functioning.

**H.** The disturbance is not attributable to the physiological effects of a substance (e.g., medication, alcohol) or another medical condition.

*Specify* whether:

**With dissociative symptoms:**  The individual's symptoms meet the criteria for posttraumatic stress disorder and, in addition, in response to the stressor, the individual experiences persistent or recurrent symptoms of either of the following:

1. **Depersonalization:** Persistent or recurrent experiences of feeling detached from, and as if one were an outside observer of, one's mental processes or body (e.g., feeling as though one were in a dream; feeling a sense of unreality of self or body or of time moving slowly).

2. **Derealization:** Persistent or recurrent experiences of unreality of surroundings (e.g., the world around the individual is experienced as unreal, dreamlike, distant, or distorted).

**Note:** To use this subtype, the dissociative symptoms must not be attributable to the physiological effects of a substance (e.g., blackouts, behavior during alcohol intoxication) or another medical condition (e.g., complex partial seizures).

*Specify* if:

**With delayed expression:**  If the full diagnostic criteria are not met until at least 6 months after the event (although the onset and expression of some symptoms may be immediate).

## POST TRAUMATIC STRESS DISORDER FOR CHILDREN 6 YEARS AND YOUNGER DSM-5

**A.** In children 6 years and younger, exposure to actual or threatened death, serious injury, or sexual violence in one (or more) of the following ways:

1. Directly experiencing the traumatic event(s).

**2.** Witnessing, in person, the event(s) as it occurred to others, especially primary caregivers.
**Note:** Witnessing does not include events that are witnessed only in electronic media, television, movies, or pictures.

**3.** Learning that the traumatic event(s) occurred to a parent or caregiving figure.

**B.** Presence of one (or more) of the following intrusion symptoms associated with the traumatic event(s), beginning after the traumatic event(s) occurred:

**1.** Recurrent, involuntary, and intrusive distressing memories of the traumatic event(s).
**Note:** Spontaneous and intrusive memories may not necessarily appear distressing and may be expressed as play reenactment.

**2.** Recurrent distressing dreams in which the content and/or affect of the dream are related to the traumatic event(s).
**Note:** It may not be possible to ascertain that the frightening content is related to the traumatic event.

**3.** Dissociative reactions (e.g., flashbacks) in which the child feels or acts as if the traumatic event(s) were recurring. (Such reactions may occur on a continuum, with the most extreme expression being a complete loss of awareness of present surroundings.) Such trauma-specific reenactment may occur in play.

**4.** Intense or prolonged psychological distress at exposure to internal or external cues that symbolize or resemble an aspect of the traumatic event(s).

**5.** Marked physiological reactions to reminders of the traumatic event(s).

**C.** One (or more) of the following symptoms, representing either persistent avoidance of stimuli associated with the traumatic event(s) or negative alterations in cognitions and mood associated with the traumatic event(s), must be present, beginning after the event(s) or worsening after the event(s):

### Persistent Avoidance of Stimuli

**1.** Avoidance of or efforts to avoid activities, places, or physical reminders that arouse recollections of the traumatic event(s).

**2.** Avoidance of or efforts to avoid people, conversations, or interpersonal situations that arouse recollections of the traumatic event(s).

### *Negative Alterations in Cognitions*

    **3.** Substantially increased frequency of negative emotional states (e.g., fear, guilt, sadness, shame, confusion).

    **4.** Markedly diminished interest or participation in significant activities, including constriction of play.

    **5.** Socially withdrawn behavior.

    **6.** Persistent reduction in expression of positive emotions.

**D.** Alterations in arousal and reactivity associated with the traumatic event(s), beginning or worsening after the traumatic event(s) occurred, as evidenced by two (or more) of the following:

    **1.** Irritable behavior and angry outbursts (with little or no provocation) typically expressed as verbal or physical aggression toward people or objects (including extreme temper tantrums).

    **2.** Hyper vigilance.

    **3.** Exaggerated startle response.

    **4.** Problems with concentration.

    **5.** Sleep disturbance (e.g., difficulty falling or staying asleep or restless sleep).

**E.** The duration of the disturbance is more than 1 month.

**F.** The disturbance causes clinically significant distress or impairment in relationships with parents, siblings, peers, or other caregivers or with school behavior.

**G.** The disturbance is not attributable to the physiological effects of a substance (e.g., medication or alcohol) or another medical condition.

*Specify* whether:

**With dissociative symptoms:**  The individual's symptoms meet the criteria for posttraumatic stress disorder, and the individual experiences persistent or recurrent symptoms of either of the following:

    **1. Depersonalization:** Persistent or recurrent experiences of feeling detached from, and as if one were an outside observer of, one's mental processes or body (e.g., feeling as though one were in a dream; feeling a sense of unreality of self or body or of time moving slowly).

**2. Derealization:** Persistent or recurrent experiences of unreality of surroundings (e.g., the world around the individual is experienced as unreal, dreamlike, distant, or distorted).

**Note:** To use this subtype, the dissociative symptoms must not be attributable to the physiological effects of a substance (e.g., blackouts) or another medical condition (e.g., complex partial seizures).

*Specify* if:

**With delayed expression:** If the full diagnostic criteria are not met until at least 6 months after the event (although the onset and expression of some symptoms may be immediate).

### PTSD Assessment Instruments

There are numerous instruments that assess PTSD, either for trauma in a broad sense, or for specific traumas such as child abuse, torture, rape, or combat experiences. The Structured Clinical Interview (SCID) DSM-IV developed by First, et al. (1997), contains the most popular PTSD module that covers a broad range of populations. A new Structural Clinical Interview (SCID) DSM-5 is completed in draft form but not yet available. Some insurance companies will allow the DSM-IV to be used until October 31, 2015, however, it's likely that most clinicians will switch to the DSM-5 and perhaps use both the DSM-IV and DSM-5 criteria during the transition process. Although the SCID DSM-IV has been excellent in the past for diagnostic purposes, it does not assist in monitoring the progress in symptom change. Many researchers and therapists are now recognizing the excellence of the Clinician Administered PTSD Scale (CAPS) by Weathers et al., (2013) DSM-5, which serves as a diagnostic tool for PTSD, and measures/monitors the severity of symptoms and the accompanying progress. The World Health Organization World Mental Health, (2004) Composite International Diagnostic Interview (CIDI) contains a PTSD module which has been used extensively, particularly for research purposes. It can be used by lay personnel as well as clinicians.

It can be beneficial to use a multimodal assessment process. For instance, a client may be hesitant to reveal the full impact of the trauma to a clinician. A self-report scale such as the Resnick, et al., (1996) Potential Stressful Experiences Inventory (PSEI) may obtain information that wouldn't easily be shared with the clinician. This scale assesses lifetime experiences of both high and low stressors and focuses on a broad range of traumatic events. By using a variety of instruments, clinicians can more competently and adequately render an accurate diagnosis.

---

## PTSD QUIZ

This quiz will assist in evaluating your knowledge of the differences between DSM-IV-TR and DSM-5. Please read each statement and look up the answer in either DSM-IV-TR or DSM-5.

1. To fulfill the DSM-5 requirements for Criterion A, a person must have responded to the trauma with feelings of intense fear, helplessness or horror.

   True _____

   False _____

2. In DSM-5 posttraumatic stress disorder is classified as an anxiety disorder.

   True _____

   False _____

3. It is possible to fulfill Criterion B by experiencing dissociative reactions (e.g. flashbacks) in which the individual feels or acts as if the traumatic event(s) were recurring.

   True _____

   False _____

**4.** If children experience frightening dreams without recognizable content, they have fulfilled the DSM-5 Criterion B for PTSD.

True _____

False _____

**5.** A person must experience 2 of the 5 symptoms in Criterion B to fulfill the requirements of that portion of the diagnostic assessment.

True _____

False _____

**6.** The first and second symptoms of Criterion C deal with persistent avoidance.

True _____

False _____

**7.** A person must experience 1 of the 7 symptoms in Criterion D which deals with negative alterations in cognitions and mood to fulfill that portion of the assessment.

True _____

False _____

**8.** If a person experiences hyper vigilance and exaggerated startle response, they have met the requirements of Criterion E which deals with marked alteration in arousal and reactivity associated with the traumatic event.

True _____

False _____

> **9.** The symptoms in Criterion B, C, D and E must last for 2 weeks before a PTSD diagnosis can be made.
>
> True _____
>
> False _____
>
> **10.** A mild disturbance in functioning is sufficient to fulfill Criterion G.
>
> True _____
>
> False _____

## QUIZ ANSWERS

**1.** False

The DSM-IV-TR Criterion A2 required that individuals experience feelings of intense fear, helplessness or horror after a traumatic event as a basis for a diagnosis of PTSD. The criterion has been changed in DSM-5 and such feelings are covered (along with other feelings) in Criterion D.

**2.** False

The DSM-IV-TR classified PTSD as an anxiety disorder; however, in the DSM-5 it is under a new classification titled Trauma- and Stressor-Related Disorders.

**3.** True

Criterion B deals with 5 intrusive symptoms which can be experienced after a traumatic event. Number 3 (experiencing dissociative reactions), is one of those symptoms and it takes only one symptom to fulfill the criteria for B.

**4.** True

Another intrusive symptom associated with the trauma is recurrent distressing dreams. With adults, the dream's content and/or affects are related to the trauma. However, children may experience frightening dreams which are caused by the trauma, but the content may not be recognizable as trauma-based.

**5.** False

A person only needs to experience one of the intrusive symptoms to fulfill Criterion B. They may experience more but only one is required as a diagnostic criterion.

**6.** True

Persistent avoidance of trauma-related stimuli is stated in DSM-5 as follows. 1. Avoidance of or efforts to avoid distressing memories, thoughts, or feelings about or closely associated with the traumatic event, 2. Avoidance of or efforts to avoid external reminders (people, places, conversations, activities, objects, situations) that arouse distressing memories, thoughts, or feelings about or closely associated with the traumatic event(s).

**7.** False

A person must experience two negative alterations in cognitions and mood to fulfill Criterion D in DSM-5.

**8.** True

Two out of the seven symptoms in Criterion D are required for fulfillment. Therefore: 1. hyper vigilance and, 2. exaggerated startle response are sufficient.

**9.** False

Duration of the disturbance which is discussed in DSM-5 Criteria B, C, D, and E is more than a month.

**10.** False

DSM-5 Criterion G states that the disturbance causes clinically significant distress or impairment in social, occupational, or other important areas of functioning.

## ACUTE STRESS DISORDER DSM-IV-TR

Acute stress disorder (ASD) entered the DSM-IV-TR as an additional entity so that clinicians could provide an early diagnosis during the first month following a trauma and to acknowledge the severity of these symptoms (APA, 2000). The symptoms must last at least 2 days and not more than 4 weeks. Essentially, DSM-5 uses the same DSM-IV-TR criteria as for posttraumatic stress disorder, except the person only needs to experience one symptom from each of the PTSD clusters of re-experiencing, avoidance, and hyper arousal. After the initial month, clients should be reevaluated to determine if their symptoms would warrant the diagnosis of PTSD. In ASD, there is greater emphasis on dissociation and three dissociative symptoms must be present for a diagnosis of ASD. A client doesn't have to experience dissociative symptoms for a diagnosis of DSM-IV-TR PTSD, but they must exhibit them for a diagnosis of ASD. The following five DSM-IV-TR dissociative symptoms are used to evaluate ASD:

1. A subjective sense of numbing, detachment, or absence of emotional responsiveness

2. A reduction in awareness of his or her surroundings (e.g., *'being in a daze'*)

3. Derealization

4. Depersonalization

5. Dissociative amnesia (i.e., inability to recall an important aspect of the trauma)

## ACUTE STRESS DISORDER DSM-5

### *Diagnostic Criteria* **308.3** (F43.0)

A. Exposure to actual or threatened death, serious injury, or sexual violation in one (or more) of the following ways:

1. Directly experiencing the traumatic event(s).

2. Witnessing, in person, the event(s) as it occurred to others.

3. Learning that the event(s) occurred to a close family member or close friend. **Note:** In cases of actual or threatened death of a family member or friend, the event(s) must have been violent or accidental.

4. Experiencing repeated or extreme exposure to aversive details of the traumatic event(s) (e.g., first responders collecting human remains; police officers repeatedly exposed to details of child abuse).

**Note:** This does not apply to exposure through electronic media, television, movies, or pictures, unless this exposure is work-related.

B. Presence of nine (or more) of the following symptoms from any of the five categories of intrusion, negative mood, dissociation, avoidance, and arousal, beginning or worsening after the traumatic event(s) occurred:

### Intrusion Symptoms

1. Recurrent, involuntary, and intrusive distressing memories of the traumatic event(s).

    **Note:** In children, repetitive play may occur in which themes or aspects of the traumatic event(s) are expressed.

2. Recurrent distressing dreams in which the content and/or affect of the dream are related to the event(s).

    **Note:** In children, there may be frightening dreams without recognizable content.

3. Dissociative reactions (e.g., flashbacks) in which the individual feels or acts as if the traumatic event(s) were recurring. (Such reactions may occur on a continuum, with the most extreme expression being a complete loss of awareness of present surroundings.) Note: In children, trauma-specific reenactment may occur in play.

4. Intense or prolonged psychological distress or marked physiological reactions in response to internal or external cues that symbolize or resemble an aspect of the traumatic event(s).

### Negative Mood

5. Persistent inability to experience positive emotions (e.g., inability to experience happiness, satisfaction, or loving feelings).

### Dissociative Symptoms

6. An altered sense of the reality of one's surroundings or oneself (e.g., seeing oneself from another's perspective, being in a daze, time slowing).

7. Inability to remember an important aspect of the traumatic event(s) (typically due to dissociative amnesia and not to other factors such as head injury, alcohol, or drugs).

## Avoidance Symptoms

8. Efforts to avoid distressing memories, thoughts, or feelings about or closely associated with the traumatic event(s).

9. Efforts to avoid external reminders (people, places, conversations, activities, objects, situations) that arouse distressing memories, thoughts, or feelings about or closely associated with the traumatic event(s).

## Arousal Symptoms

10. Sleep disturbance (e.g., difficulty falling or staying asleep, restless sleep).

11. Irritable behavior and angry outbursts (with little or no provocation), typically expressed as verbal or physical aggression toward people or objects.

12. Hyper vigilance.

13. Problems with concentration.

14. Exaggerated startle response.

C. Duration of the disturbance (symptoms in Criterion B) is 3 days to 1 month after trauma exposure.

**Note:** Symptoms typically begin immediately after the trauma, but persistence for at least 3 days and up to a month is needed to meet disorder criteria.

D. The disturbance causes clinically significant distress or impairment in social, occupational, or other important areas of functioning.

E. The disturbance is not attributable to the physiological effects of a substance (e.g., medication or alcohol) or another medical condition (e.g., mild traumatic brain injury) and is not better explained by brief psychotic disorder.

## PROLONGED GRIEF DISORDER (PGD)

Holly Prigerson, et al. (1995) (1999) (2007) met with specialists in the fields of trauma and bereavement, and as a group, it was decided that an additional disorder should be proposed for inclusion in the next DSM. They decided on the name prolonged grief disorder (PGD) for this entity. Although PGD was not included in the new DSM-5, it still warrants our attention and recognition. At present, there is no acknowledgement of grief leaving the realms of normalcy and becoming a clinically recognized diagnosis. Many clinicians believe that some types of grief can be classified as a mental disorder.

**Criterion A: Bereavement**

1. The reaction has to follow a significant loss.

**Criterion B: Separation Distress**
The bereaved person must experience at least one of three separation distress symptoms, such as:

1. Intrusive thoughts related to the deceased.
2. Intense pangs of separation distress.
3. Distressingly long yearnings for that which was lost.

**Criterion C: Cognitive, Emotional and Behavioral Symptoms**
The bereaved person must experience five of the following nine symptoms daily or to an intense or disruptive degree:

1. Feeling emotionally numb.
2. Feeling stunned or shocked.
3. Feeling that life is meaningless.
4. Confusion about one's role in life, or diminished sense of self.
5. Mistrust of others.
6. Difficulty accepting the loss.
7. Avoidance of the reality of the loss.
8. Bitterness over the loss.
9. Difficulty moving on with life.

**Criterion D: Duration**
Symptomatic disturbance must endure at least 6 months.

**Criterion E: Impairment**

It must cause clinically significant distress or impairment in social, occupational, or other important areas of functioning that represents a decrement from the person's normal (e.g., pre-loss) level of functioning.

Dr. Prigerson (2007) explains the timing as to when a diagnosis of PGD can be made and the types of losses that could cause PGD.

> The criteria for PGD specify that the particular symptomatic distress <u>must persist for at least 6 consecutive months</u>, regardless of when those 6 months occur in relation to the loss. Hence, chronic and delayed subtypes of grief could both fit within this conceptualization of PGD, as long as the chronicity and delay each include at least 6 months of symptomatic distress. More commonly, however, people diagnosed with PGD do not experience delays in the onset of symptoms post-loss. It is much more often the case among those struggling with PGD that their grief has been intense and unrelenting since the death. Although the criteria we propose here were tested for bereavement, because grief is a response to the loss of something cherished, the criteria may well apply to other significant losses apart from death (e.g., divorce, loss of pets, terminal illness). Future research will need to validate the performance of the proposed criteria with respect to these other types of losses.

Although PGD was not included in the DSM-5, it certainly merits our attention, and many clinicians believe that some grief warrants rises to the level of a disorder.

## COMPLEX POST TRAUMATIC STRESS DISORDER

Judith Herman (1992), who developed complex posttraumatic stress disorder, postulates that particular groups of trauma survivors should be diagnosed with complex posttraumatic stress disorder (CPTSD). She states that there are three cardinal symptoms that characterize complex posttraumatic stress disorder:

1. *Somatization*
2. *Dissociation*
3. *Affect dysregulation*

Dr. Bessel van der Kolk et al., (1996) states that complex PTSD is found particularly in survivors of childhood abuse, less in those abused in adolescence or adulthood, rarely in people who endured a single trauma not of human design. Moreover, these three groups of above mentioned symptoms were highly inter-correlated.

Socially speaking, there has been great violence against women and girls and it is predominantly these clients who suffer from complex PTSD. This trauma against women and girls is always relational. The victim is in a state of captivity under the control and domination of the perpetrator. How does someone establish dominance? Threats, control of bodily functions, capricious enforcement of petty rules and random intermittent rewards, isolating the victim, forcing the victim to engage in activities that are degrading or immoral. They humiliate the victim and undermine the victim's closest relationships. Bowlby (1980a) states that there are certain characterological changes in the victim.

### Characterological Changes

1. *Survivor's self-loathing*
2. *Deep mistrust of others*
3. *The template for relational reenactments that the survivor carries into adult life*

The characterological features of complex PTSD make sense if you imagine how a child would develop where the strong do as they please, the weak submit, caretakers seem willfully blind and there is no one to turn to for protection. (Herman, 2009).

Herman states that complex PTSD is symptomatic of a broad range of disorders which sometimes mimic a personality disorder, Herman (2012). As an example, Herman believes that repeated violence such as sexual abuse in childhood frequently sets the victim up for a later diagnosis of borderline personality disorder. It is well documented that the majority of clients with that diagnosis have suffered from sexual abuse in childhood. Resick (2001) also reminds us that any of the classic symptoms of borderline personality disorder such as unstable interpersonal relationships, impulsive and potentially self-damaging behaviors, intense reactive moods or inappropriate anger, paranoid ideation, or dissociation could all have their roots in traumatic memories that create difficulties in coping.

The current diagnostic criteria for PTSD has its roots in such traumatic events as combat, natural disasters, bombings, terrorist attacks, car accidents, rapes, sexual abuse, shootings, and other horrific circumstances. These disastrous circumstances are certainly characteristic of PTSD and warrant our attention and concern. However, the occurrence may be a onetime event which is highly unlikely to be repeated in the survivor's life. Lenore Terr (1994) classifies the onetime event as Trauma I and multiple events as Trauma II. Judith Herman (1992) identifies three problem areas of multiple traumas that clearly define her criteria of complex PTSD:

> The first is symptomatic: The symptom picture in survivors of prolonged trauma often appears to be more complex, diffuse, and tenacious than in simple PTSD. The second is characterological: Survivors of prolonged abuse develop personality changes, including deformations of relatedness and identity. The third area involves the survivor's vulnerability to repeated harm, both self-inflicted and at the hands of others.

Herman (1992) has described three categories. They are the *"somatic, dissociative, and affective sequelae of prolonged trauma."* The somatic and affective conditions are nearly always present, but dissociation is also common and may be an essential survival skill, which assists in coping with the unthinkable and unbearable. Hilberman (1980), states that hyper vigilance, anxiety, and agitation are earmarks for the chronically traumatized person. Herman (1992) lists other somatic symptoms: "Tension headaches, gastrointestinal disturbances, and abdominal, back, or pelvic pain are extremely common. Survivors also frequently complain of tremors, choking sensations, or nausea."

Bessel van der Kolk (1996) in a DSM-IV field trial demonstrated that the majority of people seeking treatment for trauma-related problems have histories of multiple traumas. These problems include:

- Separation and loss
- Neglect
- Physical abuse
- Emotional abuse
- Witnessing violence
- Familial substance abuse
- Other traumas

Dr. Bessel van der Kolk states that the individuals with multiple traumas often expressed symptoms such as depression, outbursts of anger, self-destructive behavior, and feelings of shame, self-blame, and distrust which caused them to seek treatment. He observed that various other clinics performing similar trauma work noticed that their clients expressed problems with:

> Depression and self-hatred, dissociation and depersonalization, aggressive behavior against self and others, problems with intimacy, and impairment in the capacity to experience pleasure, satisfaction and fun.

Dr. Judith Herman (2014) stated that complex posttraumatic stress disorder is a distinct entity and should be treated as such. Unfortunately, the diagnostic criteria that she developed and proposed for inclusion in the DSM-5 were not accepted. In a note to Dr. Schupp (Personal communication, 2014), Dr. Herman stated the existing criteria, "seem to be pretty recognizable in many different cultures." These criteria should certainly be accepted and applied as the case demands.

Briere, (2004) and van der Kolk, (2005) noted that PTSD-based models do not explain the broad range of psychological outcomes found in many individuals who present for treatment. Many of these people were exposed to early and severe child abuse and neglect as well as experiencing later adult traumas which caused their difficulties to be much more complex and severe. They may have had PTSD but also anxiety, depression, perhaps problems with identity, affect regulation, relationships, substance abuse, dissociation, somatization, and self-injurious behaviors.

## COMPLEX POSTTRAUMATIC STRESS DISORDER CRITERIA

1. A history of subjection to totalitarian control over a prolonged period (months to years). Examples include: hostages, prisoners of war, concentration camp survivors, and survivors of some religious cults. Examples also include those subjected to totalitarian systems in sexual and domestic life, including survivors of domestic battering, childhood physical or sexual abuse and organized sexual exploitation.

2. Alterations in affect regulation, including:
   - persistent dysphoria
   - chronic suicidal preoccupation
   - self-injury

- explosive or extremely inhibited anger (may alternate)
- compulsive or extremely inhibited sexuality (may alternate)

3. Alterations in consciousness, including:
- amnesia or hyper amnesia for traumatic events
- transient dissociative episodes
- depersonalization/derealization
- reliving experiences, either in the form of intrusive posttraumatic stress disorder symptoms or in ruminative preoccupation

4. Alterations in self-perception, including:
- sense of helplessness or paralysis of initiative
- shame, guilt, and self-blame
- sense of defilement or stigma
- sense of complete difference from others (may include specialness, utter aloneness, belief no other person can understand, or nonhuman identity)

5. Alterations in perception of perpetrator, including:
- preoccupation with relationship with perpetrator (includes preoccupation with revenge)
- unrealistic attribution of total power to perpetrator (caution: victim's assessment of power realities may be more realistic than clinician's)
- idealization or paradoxical gratitude
- sense of special or supernatural relationship
- acceptance of belief system or rationalizations of perpetrator

6. Alterations in relations with others, including:
- isolation and withdrawal
- disruption in intimate relationships
- repeated search for rescuer (may alternate with isolation and withdrawal)
- persistent distrust
- repeated failure of self-protection

7. Alterations in systems of meaning including:
- loss of sustaining faith
- sense of hopelessness and despair

A clinical instrument such as Bremner's Early Trauma Inventory (ETI) (Bremner, 2000) can be useful in assessing physical, emotional, and sexual abuse in childhood, as well as other traumas. The Sanders and Becker-Lausen (1995) Child Abuse and Trauma Scale, a self-report assessment, focuses on frequency and intensity of different types of traumatic events from early childhood through adolescence. The Abusive Behavior Inventory (ABI) by Shepard, M.F. and Campbell, J.A. (1992) is a reliable instrument that assesses a wide range of domestic violence abuse. The Combat Exposure Scale (CES) developed by Keane, et al. (1989) assists in diagnosing war/combat trauma with numerous veteran populations. The Women's Wartime Stressor Scale (WWSS) (Wolfe et al., 1993) focuses on the female experiences of women veterans as well as the sexual trauma and nursing aspects of the war. These instruments concentrate on repeated long-term exposure which Judith Herman has labeled complex posttraumatic stress.

It is essential to query clients regarding the symptoms listed in the DSM-5 for PTSD, ASD, Prolonged Grief Disorder (PGD), and Herman's criteria for complex posttraumatic stress disorder. Some trauma clients are not properly diagnosed, because of an inadequate intake interview, so careful history taking is essential. In addition to interviews, diagnostic instruments, and self-report tests, a clinician may want to use the Loss/Trauma History, Loss/Grief Inventory, van der Kolk's DSM-IV Field Trial list, and the Predictors for PTSD list, as well as the DSM-5 information section on predictors. Clinicians must also evaluate for comorbid disorders, since PTSD and other trauma-related syndromes rarely travel alone.

Numerous disorders or conditions may present themselves in a disguised fashion. Much diagnostic inaccuracy occurs if a clinician doesn't assess for trauma-related issues underlying the presenting problem.

## DEVELOPMENTAL TRAUMA DISORDER

According to Dr. Bessel van der Kolk, the vast majority of trauma (80%) begins at home. Parents are the primary cause of maltreatment in children. Maltreatment profoundly impacts different areas of functioning which can continue into adulthood. For example, children exposed to alcoholism or domestic violence have insecure environments which in turn may lead to depression, various medical illnesses, and a variety of impulsive and self-destructive behaviors. The vast majority of the prison population has a history of childhood trauma. Seventy-five percent of child sexual abuse perpetrators report having themselves been sexually abused during childhood. Thus, victims grow up to be perpetrators and the cycle repeats. The Adverse Childhood Experiences Study (Felitti, 1998) proved that adverse childhood experiences have a powerful effect on adult life a half century later. Adverse childhood experiences can create "depression, suicide attempts, alcoholism, drug abuse, sexual promiscuity, domestic violence, cigarette smoking, obesity, physical inactivity, and sexually transmitted diseases." It also predisposes the individual to develop heart disease, cancer, stroke, diabetes, skeletal fractures, and liver disease. The effect of caregivers on infants and children is tremendous. Children act according to how parents treat them or respond to them. Bowlby (1980a) called this interaction an *"internal working model."* We must remember that early childhood experiences occur while the brain is developing. The baby brain needs to participate in the social information transmission that offers entry in the culture. Early patterns of attachment set the quality of what happens in adult life. Secure babies trust their emotions and thoughts in all situations. They then have the confidence that they are capable of being successful and making good things happen. Also, if a difficult situation occurs, they know they can find capable trustworthy people to help them. If a parent helps a distressed child restore a sense of safety and control then a secure bond develops between caregiver and child. If a parent doesn't provide a strong supportive response, the child may mimic parents' response, (such as helplessness or disorganization). If the parent is the source of the distrust, the child can't cope, breaks down and can't control their arousal. If the child continues to frequently associate with the parent, he or she may dissociate and be unable to comprehend what happened or to execute a plan of action. Per Dr. van der Kolk (2005):

> When caregivers are emotionally absent, inconsistent, frustrating, violent, intrusive, or neglectful, children are liable to become intolerably distressed and unlikely to develop a sense that the external environment is able to provide relief. Thus, children with insecure attachment patterns have trouble relying on others to help them, while unable to regulate their emotional states by themselves. As a result, they experience excessive anxiety, anger and longings to be taken care of.

These feelings may become so extreme as to precipitate dissociative states or self-defeating aggression. Spaced-out and hyper aroused children learn to ignore either what they feel, (their emotions), or what they perceive, (their cognitions). If children are unable to achieve a sense of control and stability, then they may have multi-problems in their adult life.

The most complex trauma occurs when parents force the child to focus on danger and survival rather than on trust and learning during the time the personality develops. If a child is prompted to think about survival, then defensive states occur. It causes the child to spend time detecting and defending against threats in all areas of life. The neural pathways are all geared toward maintaining survival.

## DIAGNOSTIC CRITERIA FOR DEVELOPMENTAL TRAUMA DISORDER*

**A.** Exposure

- Multiple or chronic exposure to one or more forms of developmentally adverse interpersonal trauma (abandonment, betrayal, physical assaults, sexual assaults, threats to bodily integrity, coercive practices, emotional abuse, witnessing violence and death).

- Subjective experience (rage, betrayal, fear, resignation, defeat, shame).

**B.** Triggered Pattern of Repeated Dysregulation in Response to Trauma Cues

Dysregulation (high or low) in presence of cues. Changes persist and do not return to baseline; not reduced in intensity by conscious awareness.

- Affective
- Somatic (physiological, motoric, medical)
- Behavioral (e.g. re-enactment, cutting)
- Cognitive (thinking that it is happening again, confusion, dissociation, depersonalization)
- Relational (clinging, oppositional, distrustful, compliant)
- Self-attribution (self-hate and blame)

---

*Reprinted with permission from van der Kolk, B.A., and (2005) Developmental Trauma Disorder. Psychiatric Annals *35*:5.

**C.** Persistently Altered Attributions and Expectancies

- Negative self-attribution
- Distrust of protective caretaker
- Loss of expectation of protection by others
- Loss of trust in social agencies to protect
- Lack of recourse to social justice/retribution
- Inevitability of future victimization

**D.** Functional Impairment

1. Educational
2. Familial
3. Peer
4. Legal
5. Vocational

## DIAGNOSTIC CONFUSION RELATED TO TRAUMA

Some theorists and researchers believe that trauma plays an important role in the etiology of many psychopathologies. The following disorders are worthy of consideration as trauma-based conditions:

- Personality disorders, i.e. antisocial, borderline, histrionic, and narcissistic
- Eating disorders
- Conduct disorder
- Obsessive-compulsive disorder
- Substance abuse disorder
- Somatization disorder
- Learning disabilities
- Dissociative identity disorder
- Severely emotionally disturbed
- Malingering
- Affective disorders
- Schizophrenia

- Panic disorders
- Bipolar disorder
- Attention deficit disorder/attention deficit hyperactivity disorder

When we consider the possibility of trauma as the possible etiology for a variety of other disorders, then it brings a whole new perspective and understanding to our diagnostic assessment. How many clients have been misdiagnosed or inadequately diagnosed because a trauma background was overlooked. Sometimes a client isn't responding to treatment because the diagnosis was incomplete and pertinent issues were not addressed. A competent clinician will always look underneath the presenting problem to uncover the hidden vestiges of trauma.

# CHAPTER THREE

 # TREATMENT ISSUES AND EXPERIENCES IN TRAUMATIC STRESS

Trauma survivors with differing diagnoses will experience traumatic stress symptoms in a variety of categories. A client doesn't need to be diagnosed with PTSD in order to manifest symptoms that are part of the DSM-5 criteria. It is also important to remember that clients may demonstrate traumatic stress symptoms not covered in the DSM-5 criteria. Clients may express mild, moderate, or severe symptomatology, and clinicians need to evaluate the broad range of possibilities that present themselves as traumatic stress reactions.

## INTRUSION (RE-EXPERIENCING)

Intrusion symptoms are a red flag in the initial assessment of PTSD since they are distinctive in nature. They are manifested in Criterion B, DSM-5.

**A.** Presence of one (or more) of the following intrusion symptoms associated with the traumatic event(s), beginning after the traumatic event(s) occurred:

1. Recurrent, involuntary, and intrusive distressing memories of the traumatic event(s).

   **Note:** In children older than 6 years, repetitive play may occur in which themes or aspects of the traumatic event(s) are expressed.

2. Recurrent distressing dreams in which the content and/or affect of the dream are related to the traumatic event(s).

   **Note:** In children, there may be frightening dreams without recognizable content.

3. Dissociative reactions (e.g., flashbacks) in which the individual feels or acts as if the traumatic event(s) were recurring. (Such reactions may occur on a continuum, with the most extreme expression being a complete loss of awareness of present surroundings.)

**Note:** In children, trauma-specific reenactment may occur in play.

4. Intense or prolonged psychological distress at exposure to internal or external cues that symbolize or resemble an aspect of the traumatic event(s).

5. Marked physiological reactions to internal or external cues that symbolize or resemble an aspect of the traumatic event(s).

A client needs to experience only one of these symptoms to meet Criterion B of the DSM-5. Recurrent and intrusive, distressing recollections of the event bombard the person with their unwelcome and undesired content, often becoming so powerful that the person can think of little else. Vivid images, sensations, and feelings are ever present, and the person has a sense of reliving the experience, in the form of illusions, hallucinations, and flashbacks, as well as nightmares related to the event. Any reminder cues, internally or externally, set the person up for physiological and psychological distress. Clients may temporarily lose touch with reality and experience a dissociative state where they respond as though they were actually reliving the traumatic event.

Debbie was the mother of two children, Tommy, age eight and Jo Anne, age six. Debbie and her husband, Carl, decided to send the children to a well-respected summer camp which began a few days before they embarked on a cruise to the Caribbean. On the second day of camp, the children were playing by a fast moving stream used for river rafting and Jo Anne got too close to the water. She slipped on the mossy bank, and fell into the swirling water where her head hit a large rock, knocking her unconscious. Tommy witnessed this scene, ran downstream, jumped in the fast moving water and frantically tried to reach his sister. His attempts failed and she drowned.

Tommy has experienced frightening dreams, nearly all related to events around water. In everyday life he was visibly frightened whenever an activity required him to be around creeks, ponds, lakes, waterfalls, swimming pools, or any accumulation of water. Even his playtime is reminiscent of his rescue attempts with his sister. When playing soldiers, he frequently sends the troops on rescue missions, perhaps to find an injured or missing soldier. When watching television, he gets agitated if the hero can't rescue the dying victim. It is easy to see that Tommy may have developed PTSD, if he fulfills the additional criteria.

Even though Debbie was absent when Jo Anne drowned, she has created vivid images of the horrific event in her mind and is bothered by them during the day. She has experienced nightmares of her little girl crashing against the rock, drowning, then continuing to be carried downstream. She has intense feelings surrounding Tommy's attempts to rescue Jo Anne and has fantasized what that experience must have felt like for him. After the funeral, a friend suggested to Debbie that it might be helpful to get away for a while, perhaps taking the cruise that was intended to be her second honeymoon. Debbie was angry at the friend's lack of sensitivity but she also became aware of a new sensation. What had been previously viewed as a pleasant event was now seen as extremely distressing, and even thinking about being surrounded by all that water brought intense physiological and psychological distress. Although only one of the five symptoms is required for Criterion B, both Tommy and Debbie have several of them, and if the additional DSM criterion is met, then they both will suffer with PTSD. Even without a diagnosis of PTSD, they are experiencing a traumatic stress reaction.

## AVOIDANCE

Avoidance of stimuli associated with the trauma and numbing of general responsiveness are the essence of Criterion C of the DSM-5.

**B.** Persistent avoidance of stimuli associated with the traumatic event(s), beginning after the traumatic event(s) occurred, as evidenced by one or both of the following:

  **1.** Avoidance of or efforts to avoid distressing memories, thoughts, or feelings about or closely associated with the traumatic event(s).
  **2.** Avoidance of or efforts to avoid external reminders (people, places, conversations, activities, objects, situations) that arouse distressing memories, thoughts, or feelings about or closely associated with the traumatic event(s).

When one has experienced a trauma that is violent, unspeakable, or horrific, it is natural to seek protection both from the memories of the current event and from potential harm of a like or similar event. Most theorists agree that withdrawing from life, isolation of the self, and avoidance of acute reminders are self-protective measures. Trauma survivors instinctively know that their physiological and psychological resources have been depleted, and they need decreased stimulation and increased rest and renewal. Just as a wounded animal retreats from normal activities to lick its wounds and heal, the trauma victim seeks respite from the now overwhelming daily burdens of life.

Some amount of avoidance is required to function in life. For instance, Richard can't focus on his son's tragic death which occurred on a climbing expedition at the same time he is conducting a business meeting. Jane cannot think about her assault and rape while teaching an adult education class. Common sense applies here, as to when, where, and how much a person avoids. Temporary avoidance for constructive reasons is healthy, total continued avoidance is unhealthy.

Barbara was on her way to meet her friend Louise for dinner when a man grabbed her on a street corner, thrust a gun in her side, took her to a deserted alleyway and raped her. Fortunately, the rapist heard approaching footsteps and ran away. Barbara pulled herself together and went home. She never filed a police report or told her husband Ted about the rape. Almost immediately Barbara became uninterested in sex and couldn't verbally express her love for Ted as she normally did. She stopped socializing with important friends, stating that she needed to spend more time at home. She especially avoided her friend Louise, since she was a significant reminder of the rape. Barbara demonstrates classic symptoms of avoidance. These defensive measures are attempts to block the awareness and pain of the experience. Barbara may even avoid counseling since she would have to talk about the event. Fortunately for Barbara, her husband Ted saw such an unwelcome, dramatic change in his previously loving and expressive wife that he insisted on counseling, which brought the problem to the light. If Barbara exhibited only the symptoms of Criterion C, she would have a trauma-based condition, not PTSD. However, if she experienced the designated criteria in the other clusters as well, it would then constitute a diagnosis of PTSD.

A common method of avoiding extreme pain in traumatic circumstances is that of psychic numbing, and it is perhaps the most common form of responses to traumatic events. Mardi Horowitz (1999) in his collection of scholarly papers quoted Lifton and Olson (1976), who worked with survivors of the Buffalo Creek flood. They describe the survivor's responses it as:

> . . . diminished capacity for feeling of all kinds—in the form of various manifestations of apathy, withdrawal, depression, and overall constriction in living . . . . That state was a defense against feeling the full impact of the overwhelming death immersion . . . . Numbing, then, is an aspect of persistent grief; of the 'half-life' defined by loss, guilt, and close at times to an almost literal identification with the dead.

Current trauma and grief theorists and therapists tell us that numbing may be a *"kissing cousin"* to denial, which frequently accompanies a significant loss in one's life. Denial serves as a protection against the overwhelming acceptance of an enormous loss and could be likened to a form of *"emotional anesthesia."* The unconscious rationale of denial may be, *"if the event isn't real, then I don't have to deal with it."* Another explanation for numbing could be the protection of the trauma membrane, which consists of hormones that only allow soothing material to enter a traumatized person's brain.

## NEGATIVE ALTERATIONS IN COGNITIONS AND MOOD

Negative alternations in cognitions and mood associated with the traumatic event are a new criterion in the DSM-5 PTSD criteria.

C. Negative alterations in cognitions and mood associated with the traumatic event(s), beginning or worsening after the traumatic event(s) occurred as evidenced by two (or more) of the following:

1. Inability to remember an important aspect of the traumatic event(s) (typically due to dissociative amnesia and not to other factors such as head injury, alcohol, or drugs).
2. Persistent and exaggerated negative beliefs or expectations about one-self, others, or the world (e.g., "I am bad," "No one can be trusted," "The world is completely dangerous," "My whole nervous system is permanently ruined.")
3. Persistent, distorted cognitions about the cause or consequences of the traumatic event(s) that lead the individual to blame himself/herself or others.
4. Persistent negative emotional state (e.g., fear, horror, anger, guilt, or shame).
5. Markedly diminished interest or participation in significant activities.
6. Feelings of detachment or estrangement from others.
7. Persistent inability to experience positive emotions (e.g., inability to experience happiness, satisfaction, or loving feelings).

Sometimes traumatized individuals have an inability to remember an important part of the trauma. Unknowing people may feel that the traumatized person is in denial when actually they are experiencing the protective effects of a trauma membrane (see page 37). The trauma membrane allows material to gradually enter the consciousness of the hurting person. Lisa was a traumatized mother whose son died from a blood clot which went to his heart. When she was asked how her son died, she simply replied, "he died with cancer," when in actuality he died from the blood clot. Her trauma membrane blocked the actual cause of death from her memory, because if she recognized that the blood clot caused his death, she then would have to question whether or not she was responsible. He was being treated with a substance that was administered through a tube inserted in the subclavian vein which was kept open with heparin, an anticoagulant, when the vein was not in use. If the heparin was not injected, blood clots could occur; however, even when properly injected, freak accidents can occur. It took the mother many months before she was able to recognize that she had faithfully administered the heparin and was not responsible for this accidental death. She certainly demonstrated the number one symptom in Criterion D—the inability to remember an important part of the traumatic event. She also experienced Criterion C, number 5, which is persistent distorted cognitions about the cause or consequences of the traumatic event. She also blamed herself for his death and stated that his death was her fault, which would fulfill symptom number two of Criterion D. For quite some time, she remained in the emotional state of guilt which is consistent with number 4 in Criterion D.

## AROUSAL

Arousal and reactivity associated with a traumatic event are common symptoms which many people experience.

**D.** Marked alterations in arousal and reactivity associated with the traumatic event(s), beginning or worsening after the traumatic event(s) occurred, as evidenced by two (or more) of the following:

1. Irritable behavior and angry outbursts (with little or no provocation) typically expressed as verbal or physical aggression toward people or objects.
2. Reckless or self-destructive behavior.
3. Hyper-vigilance.
4. Exaggerated startle response.
5. Problems with concentration.
6. Sleep disturbance (e.g., difficulty falling or staying asleep or restless sleep).

Bob came to counseling with a presenting problem of insomnia, because his lack of sleep was affecting his concentration on the job. He feared that his inadequate performance would cost him his career if he didn't improve. In reviewing his loss and trauma history, it was discovered that his wife, Jeanne, had been killed by a drunk driver who's out of control car drove onto the sidewalk where she was standing. Every time Bob would walk several blocks to his favorite restaurant, he would jump at the slightest sound of an accelerated engine, and he was always looking over his shoulder. In the office, Bob seemed on edge and snapped at his secretary over trivial annoyances. He repeatedly asked her the same questions about business matters, and couldn't remember what she told him.

Bob demonstrated several of the increased arousal symptoms, even though only two were required to fulfill Criterion E. If Bob had experienced only Criterion E symptoms, he would not have met the full criteria for PTSD, but he definitely experienced a trauma-related condition.

Increased arousal symptoms are protective measures designed to prevent another tragic circumstance. This type of anxiety carries with it a sense of imminent danger or impending doom, even when no threat exists.

Alcohol and substance abuse commonly exist as an attempt to calm the increased arousal symptoms, and clients should be monitored carefully in that regard. Clients should also be cautioned regarding the use of sympathomimetics which would aggravate an already overly aroused system. Thus, they should minimize their intake of caffeine, chocolate, tea, or caffeinated soft drinks since those items stimulate the sympathetic nervous system.

## OBSESSIVE BEHAVIORS AND COMPULSIVE RE-EXPOSURE

Traumatized individuals may feel compelled to relive their current or earlier trauma with obsessive behaviors. Judith Herman (1992) reminds us that children often re-enact the scenes of the traumatic event through repetitive actions, and this compulsion is most visible with them through their play. They repeat, repeat, and repeat the trauma in such a manner that it is usually easy to interpret its meaning. Frequently, children will provide a creative or better ending to the trauma.

Herman (1992) further explains that adults may experience the same compulsion to re-create the present or past terror in a disguised form or a literal way. Individuals may unrealistically fantasize that they can alter the end result, but in actuality, they may place themselves in a precarious position of further harm. The underlying motivation is a desire to overcome the effects of the trauma, and that desire can create compulsive behaviors and re-exposure.

Debra, a dedicated employee, was experiencing high levels of arousal after the unexpected death of her sister, and defiantly refused an assignment at work. Subsequently, her supervisor threatened her with suspension and Debra submitted her resignation. The manager of her office recommended counseling and, in that safe environment, Debra became aware that the abused child within her was resisting the sexual perpetrator of earlier years, and it was a re-enactment of that event. As an adult, she could now exert her power of refusal and walk away from the relationship, even though it could have been damaging in the current situation. Debra commented about the sense of power she experienced when she asserted herself and took care of her needs. Fortunately, her supervisor didn't accept the resignation. Had he done so, it would have placed her in dire financial straits and added additional suffering to the traumatic death of her sister. In this example, the common denominator or trigger for Debra's resignation was the underlying feeling of helplessness. The sudden death of her sister brought those helpless feelings to the forefront and Debra unknowingly responded to her supervisor as though he were the childhood perpetrator.

Margaret, a frail, middle-aged woman, had been robbed and beaten in a dark alleyway of a dangerous neighborhood, yet repeatedly insisted that she wanted to revisit the same place at the identical time of night when she was assaulted. This was her consciously chosen desire which, fortunately for Margaret, her clear thinking family and friends prohibited from happening. She felt she would be obtaining some type of victory or mastery if she could revisit the location alone and not be hurt. Revisitation could be a positive experience and is known as an in vivo technique; however, the stipulations of this therapy would dictate that the revisitation was accomplished at a safe time of day and with the proper support of protective people. Margaret's method of visiting alone in the darkness would fall into an excessive risk category rather than therapy.

Excessive risk-taking can be a complication of traumatic stress. Bremner (2002) tells us that:

> Changes in fear response systems in PTSD patients underlie the ability to correctly identify threat, as if excessive temperatures have broken a thermometer and it can no longer measure the true temperature. This means that trauma clients may place themselves in precarious positions without anticipating the harm that could befall them.

Other researchers have different opinions as to the risk-taking factor in trauma clients. Some believe that re-exposure to reminders of the traumatic event can be attempts at mastery, a method to remove themselves from a victim status.

For instance, a woman who was sexually abused as a child may thrust herself into questionable relationships.

Clients would greatly benefit from a therapist's advance warning as to the obsessive behavioral urges that operate consciously and unconsciously. Psychoeducation can serve as preventative therapy for trauma survivors that are prone to obsessive behaviors and compulsive re-exposure.

## ENERGY SHIFT

In PTSD or traumatic stress, a major shift occurs where the physical, mental, and emotional energies invested in everyday living are diverted into conscious or unconscious activities. Avoidance is one such example of an energy shift. The energy invested in normal daily affairs is now displaced as the client expends great amounts of energy in avoiding memories of the trauma. In conversation they try not to talk about it and, in general, they avoid familiar people, places, and objects. Often clients are unaware of the enormous investment of energy that is required for avoidance. Tremendous energy reserves are required to keep unprocessed material out of conscious awareness, and clients frequently find themselves in a depleted state.

The concept of *"trauma bubbles"* was originated by M. Katherine Hudgins (2002) as part of her therapeutic spiral technique. It is a graphic image developed as a shorthand symbol to use with clients to describe the experience of cut-off dissociated trauma material held in unconscious awareness. She states that:

> Trauma bubbles are encapsulated spheres of active psychological awareness that contain unprocessed experiences. These experiences are dissociated and split off from conscious awareness. Like bubbles, they can be popped unexpectedly, pouring images, sensations, sounds, smells, and tastes into awareness without words.

Psychoeducation can assist and provide clients with tools to gradually deal with the trauma. The work of Pennebaker and Campbell (2000) demonstrated that clients who attempt to suppress the intrusions of images, thoughts, dreams, and memories wind up experiencing more threatening and more frequent intrusions that extend beyond the actual trauma and may contain such content as dreadful events, death, illness, aggression, or failure.

If all physical, mental, and emotional energy resides in unprocessed material, then processing the trauma in doses that are appropriate for the client is the answer as to how to shift the energies to the present. An excellent tool for therapists to employ is the *"energy shift"* question. It monitors the client's progress by percentages, and both therapist and client benefit from the information. The client responds to the following question:

## Track the Trauma

*How much of my time, energy and efforts
are involved with the trauma?*

Clients may respond with 90–95% investment at the onset of therapy which lets the therapist know that little or no processing has occurred. As clients continue to respond to the question, or to *"track the trauma"* the percentages should decrease. Of course the implied question is of equal importance: How much of my time, energy and efforts are available for the present?

This tracking method shows the client they are making progress; they need the encouragement or the signposts of healing movement. The question also allows the therapist to know if the current therapies are working and moving the client to resolution.

## Emotional Repercussions

Trauma clients fear greatly that the emotions they may experience will be overwhelming and incapacitating. As a result of this fear, they may avoid any stimuli that would arouse these emotions. This client doesn't want to talk about the traumatic event, and may be misclassified in therapy as resistant, when in reality the individual is employing a defense mechanism. If clients avoid thinking and processing, they may feel better temporarily, even though they are lengthening the healing process. Expressing the emotions, regardless of their intensity, is essential and therapeutic, while avoidance will continue the PTSD or traumatic stress symptoms. Clients may also be tempted to turn to drugs and alcohol in an attempt to numb the feelings, which again lengthens the process by avoidance. As mentioned earlier, clinicians need to watch for signs of substance abuse which frequently accompanies intense emotional experiences.

If a client was abused as a child, then she or he may have developed dissociative identity disorder (DID), borderline personality disorder (BPD), bipolar disorder, or a myriad of other disorders mentioned earlier. There may be excessive mood swings with intense reactions. They may use risky methods of shutting down their feelings such as fast driving or promiscuity. They may view a mole hill as a mountain, and the little irritants of life may become a crisis. Self-mutilation and suicide attempts may be a way of dealing with overwhelming emotions.

Other types of emotional repercussions are observed in the early work of Robert Jay Lifton and Eric Olson, (1976). They both worked with survivors of the Buffalo Creek, West Virginia flood disaster and observed that images and memories of the horror were still vivid two-and-a-half years after the event; these were indelible images that threatened to be permanent.

Some trauma survivors will suffer from what Lifton and Olson (1976) termed *"death imprint"* and *"death anxiety."* The death imprint *"consists of memories and images of the disaster, invariably associated with death, dying, and mass destruction."*

Lifton and Olson explain that *death anxiety* is apparent when *what was "unnatural" becomes "natural."* In other words, survivors expect other loved ones to die; a little stimulus such as rain in their case set up this pattern of expectations. The death anxiety was also manifested through terrifying dreams where the survivor was struggling to remain alive.

*"Death guilt"* was also present in that survivors condemned themselves for living while others had died. Connected to this guilt may be the failure of the survivor to save the deceased. Anger at self as well as at others who are perceived at fault is also common. These survivors are always searching for the answers to the *unanswerable question: "Why did I survive and my loved ones die?"* More currently, we see this phenomenon with the Oklahoma City bombing, the September 11th attack, the Amish shootings, the Columbine shootings, and the Aurora theater shootings, among others.

Since trauma memories are accompanied by intense emotions, survivors may plan their lives in ways that avoid such intrusion. Researchers van der Kolk and Ducey (1989) state that drugs or alcohol temporarily numb awareness as does dissociation which blocks conscious awareness. Clients need to learn to use physiological techniques such as meditation, breathing, and relaxation to restore their depleted resources rather than self-destructive measures. Medication is often required as well.

## INFORMATION PROCESSING

Trauma survivors experience internal stress and turmoil, frequently unconsciously, and it restricts their ability to process information. Though they need to attend to present day responsibilities, their energies may be absorbed by areas of unprocessed trauma. One evidence of unprocessed memories is the experience of amnesia. Henry Krystal (1968) examined some

Holocaust survivors and explained that: *"No trace of registration of any kind is left in the psyche; instead, a void, a hole, is found."* It is no wonder that survivors experience sights and sensations in the present, yet as van der Kolk and Fisler (1995) have stated, there is no way the survivor can make sense out of what they are feeling or seeing. Since much cognitive and emotional energy is absorbed with the unprocessed material, very little energy is available for the tasks of ordinary living.

The term *"biased perception"* has been used by van der Kolk and Ducey (1989) and McFarlane, Weber, and Clark (1993) to explain that trauma survivors react, "preferentially to trauma related triggers at the expense of being able to attend to other perceptions. As a consequence, they have smaller repertoires of neutral or pleasurable internal and environmental sensations that could be restitutive and gratifying."

Some intrusive elements of trauma may be easy to identify at first, but as van der Kolk (1996) reminds us, they may become increasingly more subtle and expand to more generalized areas. He explains that: *"What should be irrelevant stimuli may become reminders of the trauma."*

Roger's supervisor is a controlling hyperactive man and in his haste, he often gives confusing and sometimes conflicting instructions. Roger calmly questions and clarifies the supposed contradictions and has been able to perform satisfactorily in this environment for 15 years. He loves his job, as well as his co-workers. Unfortunately, Roger's brother, Harold, became ill and during the course of his treatment in the hospital, he was given a drug to which he had a known allergic reaction. The hospital nurse had duly recorded the drugs to which he was allergic, but the illegible notes were obscure. Since the drug in question was usually prescribed for his condition, it was administered to Harold and he died from an extreme allergic reaction. Roger took 2 weeks off from work and after that time he thought he could resume his duties. He decided that returning to work would return some sense of normalcy to his life. At least, his days were unchanged and he anticipated his work as therapeutic. However, the resumption of his duties did not turn out as expected. Although everyone was caring and supportive, Roger became increasingly tense, nervous, and irritated with his supervisor and co-workers. Only when he worked with a trauma specialist was he able to view his supervisor's lack of clarity, precision, and accuracy as a reminder of the confused prescription that caused his brother's untimely death. In fact, Roger had generalized the confusion stimulus to everyone he knew. He couldn't tolerate the least bit of confusion and began to withdraw from other co-workers, thus minimizing the occurrence of any confusion. In therapy, the unconscious became conscious, which greatly disempowered his accompanying responses and need to isolate.

Trauma survivors have memories that operate differently from normal memories which consist of verbal sequential processing. Frequently the memories are encoded pictorially without the assistance of words. The client may not be able to find words to express the horror of the experience. Judith Herman (1992) states that, "traumatic memories lack verbal narrative and context; rather, they are encoded in the form of vivid sensations and images. . . . In their absence of verbal narrative, traumatic memories resemble the memories of young children."

Most children under two-and-one-half years of age cannot verbalize traumatic events, yet they are indelibly encoded in memory (Herman, 1992).

Bessel van der Kolk and Alexander C. McFarlane (1996) have summarized the six critical issues concerning information processing with PTSD sufferers:

1. Persistent intrusive trauma memories which interferes with attentiveness to incoming information

2. Compulsive exposure to situational reminders of the trauma

3. Specific avoidance of trauma-related emotions and generalized numbing of responsiveness

4. Inability to modulate physiological responses to generalized stress

5. Problems with attention distractibility and stimulus discrimination

6. Alterations in psychological defense mechanisms and in personal identity which changes their perception as to what new information is relevant.

## THE FRAGMENTATION OF THE SELF

In trauma, the self may experience various levels of fragmenting, splintering, or shattering. The type of trauma a person encounters determines the degree of the damage to the self. For instance, if a person's trauma has been enacted at the hand of a perpetrator, then the fragmentation will be worse. The more control a perpetrator exerts over a victim, the more fragmentation the victim will experience. In prolonged repeated abuse, the perpetrator's intent is that of *"breaking"* the victim which means the annihilation of a sense of self. This breaking is also known as *"soul murder."*

---

Six Critical Issues with PTSD suffers is reprinted by permission from Traumatic Stress (©1996). Guilford Publications.

Hearst and Moscow (1982) and Lovelace and McGrady (1980) describe the effects of some totalitarian systems be they sexual, domestic, political, religious, or otherwise, and explain that even the victim's name may be removed. In some situations, they may be given a number which provides some record of their existence; in other environments, they are nameless and numberless, reduced to a nonentity status. Lovelace and McGrady (1980) and Timerman (1981) tell us that survivors may refer to themselves as a *"nonhuman life form."* There is a vast difference in self descriptions between the victim of a single acute trauma and a victim of chronic trauma. Herman (1992) indicates the one-time victim may say she is "not herself" since the occurrence of the trauma. The victim of chronic trauma may not believe *that she has a self.* Krystal and Niederland (1968) noted that concentration camp survivors demonstrated numerous changes regarding their personal identity. Most of the survivors indicated they were a different person; however, those who suffered the more extreme forms of abuse stated that they were not a person.

Childhood abuse produces many distortions and alterations of the self. Abused children develop even more complicated versions of an identity crisis than concentration camp survivors. The concentration camp survivors never had the initial trust issues with the perpetrator that the child did. They expected *"the enemy to be the enemy."* Quite a different scenario was in place for the child. The very people upon whom the child was dependent, the ones who were supposed to protect and nurture, were the enemy. It is no surprise that numerous psychiatric disorders have their origin in childhood trauma such as dissociative identity disorder and borderline personality disorder.

Often the victimized child views the self as ugly, sinful, defiled, contaminated, ruined, or guilty to name a few of the labels of the distorted selves. Although this is a milder form of distortion, it is pervasive and invades all aspects of the survivor's life. We know that beliefs predict behavior, and that a child's perception is his reality, so the lifestyle follows those predictions. Early interventions in children are vital so as to disrupt the formation of damaging beliefs, perceptions, and behaviors.

Horowitz (1999) provides a warning and some advice regarding the impact of traumatic events on identity. Trauma can:

> Lead to a variety of self-concept disturbances such as identity diffusion (a chaotic sense of self-fragmentation) or depersonalization. To bolster a sense of identity during stress, an individual often turns

for reflectance of self to others. Attachment and bonding impulses are heightened. In such instances, victims may even bond with their aggressors if they are isolated from better sources of support. This can lead to dissociative experiences, in which the aggressor is bad, and in which the aggressor is good. Such segregations of person schematization make it harder to work over and work through memories and fantasies of traumatic events.

Clinicians definitely need to encourage healthy support systems for trauma survivors, as well as being an ideal one. In addition, counselors must watch for dangerous bonding activities with perpetrators, while treating and bringing the client into wholeness.

## DISSOCIATION

Numbing is a form of dissociation, and it also depletes energy reserves. It takes much energy to suppress emotions. Fear that the emotion might be too overwhelming can cause a person to numb or dissociate. The attempt here is to block undesirable emotions but, as in a major depressive episode, a client cannot just block the traumatic pain, they numb all emotions, positive or negative. Williams and Poijula (2002) list the detrimental impact of numbing the emotions in their PTSD Workbook.

1. Blunted emotional and physical pain, pleasure, and responsiveness; loss of interest in the world and things that previously brought pleasure to you

2. Inability to discriminate between pain and pleasure (when you do not feel emotions, it is easier for you to be re-victimized)

3. Poor memory; clouded thinking

4. Lack of emotional responsiveness leading to feelings of shame and the belief that one is shameful

5. Increased need for stimulants and stimulation in order to feel alive; tendency to take risks of all kinds to create excitement and counteract the dead feeling inside you

---

Numbing emotions is reprinted with permission from The PTSD Workbook (© 2002). New Harbinger Publications.

6. Self-mutilating as a way to feel alive

7. Episodes of panic and rage

8. Retreating from life

9. Letting your emotional and physical reactions guide you

10. Feeling detached from others

11. Being unable to experience life because you feel empty inside

12. Having no interest in sex; having sexual dysfunction

13. Having no energy; feeling apathetic (not caring) and lethargic (being tired all the time)

14. Experiencing mental sluggishness

Dissociation provides a distancing step that serves as a defense mechanism. If clients mentally step outside the realms of the trauma, then they aren't as close to it and it doesn't hurt as much. Clinicians will frequently observe their clients using denial and dissociation to soothe the pain.

Sometimes dissociative symptoms appear similar to psychotic episodes and disorders. It is relatively easy to differentiate between dissociative symptomatology and psychotic symptomatology. If a client's narrative descriptions, visual or auditory hallucinations, or olfactory senses are related *only* to the trauma, it would not be considered a psychosis. Familiarity of any form with the trauma is indicative of a person suffering from PTSD. With psychosis, there is usually no familiarity with the content. The patient may hear a strange voice or visualize a bizarre scene, but it doesn't have to be reminiscent of the trauma. *Relatedness to the trauma becomes a key element for diagnosing dissociative symptomatology and distinguishing it from a psychotic episode.*

One of the most extreme forms of fragmentation manifests as dissociative identity disorder, (DID), formerly named multiple personality disorder. The American Psychiatric Association changed the name to focus on the identity fragmentation. Bremner (2002) reminds us that it may be a wiser choice to refer to *"identity fragments"* in a client as opposed to separate or multiple personalities. These identity fragments may have been given a name, but they are not complete personalities, they are all part of the person. Putnam, et al. (1986) has shown that nearly all cases of DID are a result of early child abuse.

Clients with DID are frequently in a dissociative state, however, in contrast, the client with borderline personality disorder (BPD) never dissociates. Nonetheless, the client with BPD lives on a fine line between normal adaptive functioning and psychic disability. Herman (1992) points out that people with BPD possess an unstable sense of self, and Kernberg (1967) felt that the splitting of inner representations of self was a dominant feature of this disorder. Herman (1992) reminds us that even though clients with a BPD diagnosis don't dissociate, they do have difficulty in the formation of an integrated identity. Rieker and Carmen (1986) explain the self of abused children as a *"disordered and fragmented identity deriving from accommodations to the judgment of others."* Society definitely needs to invest more resources, time, and efforts into prevention and early treatment of child abuse, and clinicians need to thoroughly evaluate abuse issues when diagnosing children.

Dissociation is a common experience among traumatized people, especially those who have been involved in multiple traumas or have a diagnosis of complex PTSD. Dissociation is a survival mechanism used to remove and protect the self from perceived threats and painful feelings. There are numerous forms of dissociation, five of which are listed in the DSM-IV-TR diagnosis of Acute Stress Disorder:

1. A subjective sense of numbing, detachment, or absence of emotional responsiveness
2. A reduction in awareness of his or her surroundings (e.g., 'being in a daze')
3. Derealization—a perception that the person has lost contact with external reality
4. Depersonalization—a feeling of loss of self or personal identity, delirium
5. Dissociative amnesia (i.e. inability to recall an important aspect of the trauma)

The DSM-5 has a separate chapter for dissociative disorders. It follows the Trauma-and Stressor-Related Disorders chapter. The intention of the chapters being next to each other is to demonstrate the close relationship between these diagnostic disorders. This chapter in the DSM-5 includes the following:

1. Dissociative identity disorder
2. Dissociative amnesia
3. Depersonalization/derealization disorder
4. Other specified dissociative disorder
5. Unspecified dissociative disorder

DID is one of the most extreme forms of fragmentation. The criteria required for a diagnosis of DID are the presence of two or more distinct personality states or an experience of possession. Sustained periods of identity disruption may occur when psychosocial pressures are severe or prolonged. Recurrent memory gaps of everyday events, important personal information, and/or traumatic events, that are inconsistent with ordinary forgetting, is also important in diagnosing DID.

Dissociative amnesia is an inability to recall autobiographical information that's inconsistent with normal forgetting. A person may experience a gap in time where an event or a specific aspect of an event has disappeared from their memory. For example, Mary may have gone to a different state to visit her sister and is not able to recall the 2 days that she spent there.

Depersonalization/derealization disorder is linked together in the DSM-5 whereas the two disorders were identified separately in the DSM-IV-TR. The dual definition defines it as clinically significant persistent or recurrent depersonalization (i.e., experiences of unreality or detachment from one's mind, self, or body and/or derealization (i.e., experiences of unreality or detachment from one's surrounding). Simply said depersonalization removes the person from the self and derealization causes them to lose contact with reality. Some of our military forces exhibit the problem of depersonalization. If they are prisoners of war, they may view themselves as a number or as a statistic, rather than a real, live person. Some have expressed themselves in terms such as *"I'm a non-human life form."* Obviously, this is a severe form and there are various degrees of detachment from the self. In the event of derealization, let's suppose Mary is standing on a street corner and she loses contact as to where she is and what she is doing. She is attempting to cross the street and steps in front of an oncoming car and is seriously injured.

Other specified dissociative disorder applies to individuals who have some characteristics of a dissociative disorder but do not meet the full criteria for a specific disorder. Bill is an example in that he was tortured and brain-washed while a prisoner of war and he had identity disturbance or some other manifestation of radically different beliefs. Other individuals may have transient conditions that typically last less than a month, or maybe just a few days or hours. This disorder is an acute dissociative reaction to a stressful event.

Unspecified dissociative disorder applies when the individual does not meet the full criteria of any dissociative disorder but has some of the symptoms that cause distress. This category is used when the clinician chooses not to specify the reason that the criteria aren't met. Usually there is insufficient information to make a more specific diagnosis. Perhaps Steve becomes forgetful when he enters his child's bedroom because his little girl died a tragic death in her bedroom. The forgetfulness occurs only in that particular room therefore rendering a more specific diagnostic decision is impossible.

Dissociation is closely linked with the DSM-5 PTSD criterion C, which refers to persistent avoidance to stimuli associated with the traumatic event. Trauma triggers (people, places, objects that are reminders of the trauma) can lead to a dissociative event. Perhaps individuals with complex PTSD have more difficulty with various forms of dissociation due to the horrendous traumas they have experienced. The more severe traumas that culminate in complex PTSD cause more of the various forms of dissociation. Many sexually abused women have fallen prey to *"learned helplessness"* and they dissociate from their body as a way to bear the unbearable.

Traumatic amnesia could also be viewed as dissociation. It is a total repression of the memories connected to the trauma. Often feelings of physical symptoms remain but the trauma is not a conscious memory. Treatments such as eye movement desensitization reprocessing (EMDR), which is discussed later, can be helpful to remove the remnants or cellular memories of the trauma. In our fourth chapter of treatments, we shall discuss other more current remedies. All physical movement such as exercise, dancing, yoga, Tai Chi, etc. will assist in healing these unconscious cellular memories.

## ATTACHMENT THEORY

Born with limited capacities for self-regulation, human infants are dependent on the externally mediated interactive regulation of their primary attachment figures to maintain their arousal within the window of tolerance, Corrigan, et al. (2011). Whether that attachment relationship is consistent or inconsistent, secure or insecure, it provides the context within which the infant develops lifelong tendencies for regulating arousal and affect. Early disruptions in attachment have enduring detrimental effects, diminishing the capacity to moderate arousal, develop healthy relationships and cope with stress.

Early attachment needs are expressed as bodily-based needs. Touch is the first interaction immediately after birth. It is the first form of communication between the baby and its primary attachment system. Visual and auditory functions become stronger as time goes on. Attachment is based on caregiver's concise and accurate attunement to infant: physical handling, feeding, soothing, crying, laughing, cooing, holding the baby, eye contact, etc.

*Arousal instead of attachment occurs if the primary attachment figure is abusive, emotionally vacant, or some "type of perpetrator."* There is no comfort or repair from supposed caregiver. In actuality, trauma can occur before birth by an attachment experience in the womb.

## TRAUMA IN THE WOMB

There is an interesting field of study called fetal origins. Life as a fetus is affected by certain factors:

1. Quality and quantity of nutrition received in the womb
2. Pollutants, drugs and infections the fetus was exposed to
3. The mother's health, stress level and state of mind and emotions while pregnant
4. Whether the baby was wanted or unwanted

These 9 months permanently influence the wiring of the brain and the functioning of organs such as the heart, liver and pancreas. The conditions we encounter in utero shape our susceptibility to disease, our appetite and metabolism, our intelligence and temperament. In the last 10 years, literature that links fetal origins to cancer, cardiovascular disease, obesity, mental illness, arthritis, osteoporosis and cognitive decline has exploded.

What a woman does daily affects the fetus:

1. The air she breathes
2. Food and drink she consumes, drugs or alcohol—(e.g., fetal alcohol syndrome)
3. Emotions she feels

The fetus incorporates these offerings into its own body, making them part of its flesh and blood. The fetus also absorbs these maternal contributions as information or as answers to questions about its survival. It is amazing to realize that a fetus can think on a primitive level.

What would you think about conquering obesity and heart disease through interventions before birth? Nobel Prize winning economist Amartya Sen co-authored a paper with Siddiq Osmani (2003) about the importance of fetal origins to a population's health and productivity. Poor prenatal experience, he wrote, "sows the seeds of ailments that afflict adults." As an example, he reiterated the robust relationship between low birth weight and cardiovascular disease.

## RESULTS OF POOR ATTACHMENT

1. Emotional instability
2. Social dysfunction
3. Poor response to stress
4. Cognitive disorganization and disorientation

The University of Dartmouth Medical School studied the integration of "hard science of infant attachment and child and adolescent brain development with sociological evidence of how civil society shapes outcomes for children," (Institute for American Values, 2003). They came to the conclusion that, "all scientific research now shows that from the time a baby is born, a baby's brain is biologically already formed to connect in relationships."

A thirty-one year study at John Hopkins Medical School sought to discover whether a single related cause existed for mental illness, hypertension, malignant tumors, coronary heart disease and suicide. The most significant predictor of these five calamities was found to be a lack of closeness to the parents, especially the father (Thomas, C.B. & Duszynski, K.R., 1974)

## THE NEUROBIOLOGY OF BROKEN ATTACHMENT BONDS

According to Allan Schore (2005), infancy is the critical period of attachment to a caregiver. During the first year of life the infant and the caregiver form an emotional communication which is a secure attachment bond. It is important to remember that PTSD can occur at any time after the first year of life. DSM-5 tells us there can be *"delayed expression"* with the recognition that some symptoms typically appear immediately and that the delay is in meeting the full criteria. Symptoms usually begin within 3 months after the trauma, but it can be months or years before the full criteria for diagnosis are met.

Allan N. Schore (2005) has extensively researched the neurobiology of broken attachment bonds. At 2 months of age, some studies show that infants respond with right hemisphere activity when exposed to a woman's face. Other studies conducted using near-infrared spectroscopy, which is the most suitable technique for studying infants, also revealed that specifically the right hemisphere of 5-month-olds responded to images of female faces.

Near-infrared spectroscopy is a neuroimaging technology that offers a relatively non-invasive, safe, portable, and low-cost method of indirect and direct monitoring of brain activity. By measuring changes in near-infrared light, it allows researchers to monitor blood flow in the front part of the brain.

The first 18 months are critical for attaching securely to primary care givers. The human limbic system myelinates in the first year and a half, which means that a child will either trust or mistrust a parent/caregiver by that time. The early maturing right hemisphere (Geschwind & Galaburda, 1987; Schore, 1994), which is connected to the limbic system (Tucker, 1992; Gainotti, 2000) is experiencing a growth spurt at this time which means that the emotional constructs for attachment are in place. In addition, attachment communications specifically impact limbic and cortical areas of the developing right cerebral brain (Henry, 1993, Schore, 1994, 2005, Siegel, 1999). The production of negative emotions can be seen in infants as young as 12 months of age and control of negative emotions is evident by 24 months.

Sieratzki and Woll (1996) tell us that touch is extremely important in developing the right hemisphere. The right side picks up nonverbal affective facial expressions, gestures and prosody. Prosody deals with right brain signals used in implicit attachment communications. If these communications do not occur during the appropriate time frames, then the person's emotional life may be affected for life. Attachment experiences shape the early organization of the right brain, the neurobiological core of the human unconsciousness (Schore 2002). Schore (2002) states that we need to focus our clinical treatment with trauma clients upon the affective dynamics of right brain insecure internal working models that are activated within the therapeutic model. Schore (2002) proposed that the, *"empathetic therapist's capacity to regulate the patient's arousal states within the affectively charged nonconscious transference-countertransference relationship is critical to clinical effectiveness."*

## HEART OF ATTACHMENT THEORY

Attachment theory focuses on two key questions:

1. *Am I worthy of love?*
2. *Are others capable of loving me?*

The answers to these questions are the basis for our core relational beliefs. They impact how we see ourselves and it shapes the way we think, feel and act. Self-definition begins in early infancy. John Bowlby (1980a), originator of attachment theory, identified two key questions:

1. *Is the self-perceived to be worthy of the primary caregivers' (Mom and/or Dad) caring response?*
2. *Is the primary caregiver perceived to be reliable and responsive to the child's needs?*

Are parents there in times of stress, need and want? If a caregiver is reliable and available during times of stress and duress, we develop positive beliefs about our worth. Then the child can say, *"I am worthy of love and I am capable of gaining love and support in times of emotional stress."* The response of the caregiver shapes our feelings about other individuals and God.

Erik Erikson's developmental psychology tells us that either trust or mistrust develops during the first year of life. Trust develops if the child cries and is comforted, mistrust occurs if the child cries and receives anger and rejection.

Based on interactions with those who are responsible for caring for them, children form perceptions about their identities, others, intimacy, and emotions as early as the first year of life. These positive or negative responses from caregivers are imprinted on mirror neurons, and later almost instinctively without awareness, the child's emotions and behaviors respond in the way the parents responded. The person may scold him or herself if laughing or being silly. They may remind themselves, *"Don't be happy. Don't love. Don't marry. Never play or waste time. Always work."* Many messages are implanted, unremembered, but later played out. These unconscious messages are extremely powerful and can control the adult without his or her knowledge.

## EXPERIENCE OF ATTACHMENT

1. **"Safe Base Security Attachment":** Secure base experience gives child a sense of security and the belief that his mother is available, attentive, accessible and loving.
2. **Child's Exploration:** He explores his surroundings and builds his confidence. Self-confidence is parent-given and begins by a secure relationship. "Seeking and searching" his environment is the next step that occurs when a child feels secure. Confidence begins by child having confidence in the parent, therefore it is relational.

3. **"Safe Base" Threatened:** If something threatens the sense of security, stronger exploration evaporates and attachment behavior is activated. The child needs to reconnect with the parent to feel safe again. This is propelled by intense emotion, usually a mixture of anxiety and anger. The child may use seeking and signaling behaviors to obtain physical closeness to the parent. The child may whine, cry, scream or plead. If Mother doesn't respond with appropriate compassion, the child concludes his mother isn't safe, doesn't care and possibly isn't worthy of his love.

4. **Safety Achieved:** The reconnection has been established, threat dissipated, love reinforced.

These memories are wired into your brain; core beliefs about relationships are encoded and organized into intense working models that are stored in the limbic system (the emotional brain) as implant memories. These memories are emotionally charged preverbal structures that influence behavior before explicit verbal communication is possible. This wiring along with personality and other factors determines the person's style of relating to others.

## ATTACHMENT STYLES

### Secure

- Positive perception of self
- Positive perception of others
- Desires intimacy in relationships
- Demonstrates healthy autonomy
- Trusts others can meet their needs

### Shaky

- Negative perception of self
- Unrealistic positive perception of others
- Can be clingy in relationships
- Doesn't have healthy autonomy
- Can't trust others to meet their needs

**Stand-Offish**

- Overly positive perception of self
- Excessively negative view of others
- Strives to avoid intimacy
- Too self-reliant
- Can't trust others to meet their needs

**Scared**

- Negative view of self
- Negative view of others
- Wants others to provide their self-worth
- Can't rely on self
- Fears others won't meet their needs

# CHAPTER FOUR

 # PHYSIOLOGICAL INTERVENTIONS

## THE IMPORTANCE OF SLEEP

Harvard psychiatrist and neurophysiologist Allan Hobson (1994) states, *"Of all the practices known to be associated with good health, sleep is the most fundamental."* Many PTSD clients report sleep disturbances particularly with nightmares related to the trauma and with heightened arousal symptoms which prohibit the client from falling asleep and staying asleep. Mellman, et al. (1995) and Inman, et al. (1990) have shown that excessive motor activity occurs while sleeping and when awake, indicating the continuous level of arousal in PTSD clients. We know that sleep has restorative value physically, mentally, and emotionally, so lack of it contributes, lengthens, and exacerbates the PTSD condition.

The awakenings during the night may interfere with rapid eye movement (REM) sleep which is known by many theorists to assist in emotional adapting to the traumatic event. REM sleep occurs at regular intervals throughout the night, providing a person with four or five REM cycles in a normal night's sleep. Kramer, et al. (1984) states that most dreaming in non-PTSD clients occurs during the REM cycles; however, nightmares experienced by PTSD clients occur during both REM and non-REM cycles. Mellman, et al. (1995), Ross, et al. (1994) and Kramer, et al. (1984) remind us that if dreams occur in non-REM sleep, they are always preceded by REM sleep.

Medication may be indicated in some cases of PTSD. Davidson, et al. (1990) has demonstrated that amitriptyline (Elavil) has a modest effect in suppressing REM cycles and it may be needed on occasion. Armitage, et al. (1994) has shown that although nefazodone (Serzone) is useful in maintaining sleep it doesn't suppress REM cycles. Clients, treated with it reported having dreams but of a less traumatic nature as compared to clients who did not receive Serzone. However, Reynolds, et al. (1990) reminds us that if REM cycles are suppressed or disrupted, there is increased pressure (reduced latency) for them to return. If individuals are deprived of REM sleep for several nights, the REM cycle will start within a few minutes after sleep begins. In normal sleep, the REM cycle doesn't occur until approximately 90 minutes after the entry to sleep. Some researchers believe that REM is required for organizing information and sorting out emotional ingredients, therefore REM cycles are needed and an essential part of healing. Of course, this is a Catch 22. If REM is beneficial, yet prevented, it may delay emotional processing and ultimate healing time. On the other hand, if a client refuses to go to sleep for fear of nightmares, then progress is also slowed and recovery delayed. These situations require the assistance of competent medical professionals and medications administered on a case by case basis. A trial-and-error approach must sometimes be applied to assist the client with insomnia.

The current best information we have on treating medical management of PTSD symptoms is with selective serotonin reuptake inhibitors (SSRIs). Many studies have been researched by the Agency for Healthcare Research & Quality, US Department of Health and Human Services, *Interventions for the prevention of post-traumatic stress disorder in adults after exposure to psychological trauma.* (2013). SSRI's have proven themselves effective in all DSM-5 categorical symptom areas related to PTSD. (Please see posttraumatic stress disorder diagnostic criteria.) Agreement among professionals on prescribing SSRIs as the first line of treatment is consistent and numerous studies Support the use of these medications.

Clinicians have known for some time that the release of serotonin and norepinephrine decline steadily across the sleep cycle (Hobson, 1994), thus leading less depletion of those essential neurotransmitters over time. One hypothesis is that PTSD symptoms are caused by the depletion of serotonin; therefore the more serotonin in the system, the fewer PTSD symptoms. Until more research occurs, medical personnel must treat cautiously and carefully and on a client by client basis.

## STRESS INOCULATION TRAINING

Stress inoculation training (SIT) consists of teaching coping skills that assist in anxiety reduction in trauma survivors' everyday life. This umbrella can be a catch-all for stress management, and the term is frequently used to cover various forms of relaxation, breath work, biofeedback, and other physiological interventions, role playing, communication techniques, assertiveness training, thought stopping, and various self-regulation techniques. Some of these areas will be covered individually.

## RELAXATION

Because of the increased arousal state that exists in many trauma survivors, the need for relaxation has heightened importance. Relaxation is person-specific, but it allows trauma survivors to engage themselves in an experience that causes them to temporarily lose track of time. The following guided imagery is a positive form of dissociation that should be encouraged.

### A. Guided Imagery

Guided imagery uses the senses in a creative manner. It bypasses the left brain, (the talking side), and uses the visual, sensory, and emotional channels that are resident in the right brain. Guided imagery heals the hyper vigilant right hemisphere and affects unconscious beliefs and thoughts. While listening to an audiotape, a client can visualize himself walking in a forest with pine needles crackling under his feet, smelling the scent of the pine, listening to a babbling brook, or seeing the brilliantly colored flowers beside the pathway. A client may want to make his own relaxation tape using whatever images work best. The familiarity of one's own voice is pleasing to the psyche and offers no resistance to the message. Since trust is a major concern with clients who have been violated by another person, they may not be comfortable allowing another individual to guide their thoughts. In this case, clients may tape their own message, saying exactly what is wanted or needed. Clients can also use soothing, comforting music in the background. Steven Porges' (2011) has definitely shown that music therapy is a powerful healing force, so its addition adds extra benefit.

Imagery can be expanded to include people who comforted the client and visualizing the manner in which the comforters cared for the client. The client may notice how they felt while visualizing that special, loving person. Sometimes God is brought into this picture, or the client is sitting in a flower garden with Jesus. There are no limitations as to what can be imaged that is helpful or comforting to the client.

### B. Progressive Relaxation

Progressive relaxation involves tensing and relaxing various muscle groups. The client may sit comfortably in a chair and start by tensing the muscles in the feet, holding it for a few seconds, then releasing. They then tense the calves in the legs for a few seconds and release. They continue to work upwards tensing and releasing each muscle group.

Since trauma survivors already feel tense much of the time, it helps them to *"go with the tension."* Accentuating the tension in different muscle groups and then relaxing each group gives them a sense of control or mastery over their physiological condition.

## C. Active Relaxation or Recreation

Active relaxation or recreation consists of any activity that temporarily absorbs the client. It could be knitting, crocheting, checkers, chess, puzzles, cards, painting, drawing, playing an instrument, gardening, walking in the park, playing football or basketball, hiking or biking, any pursuit that provides a constructive outlet for the pent-up emotional energy. Trauma survivors already experience an aroused system, so releasing that energy in a healthy way assists in the healing process.

## D. Passive Relaxation

There are some trauma survivors who will not participate in active forms of relaxation. They may benefit from something more sedate and less taxing. Passive relaxation is an involvement that requires little expenditure of energy. Perhaps a client might experiment with reading a good book, listening to favorite music, sunning in a backyard lounge chair, or watching favorite movies or television programs.

When a person has experienced a trauma, they may not want to engage in any activities, even ones that were previously considered pleasurable. It is important that they participate in some form of relaxation even if it provides only a small amount of momentary pleasure. Those tiny bits of distraction provide some reprieve from constantly focusing on the trauma, and also assist the healing process.

## EXERCISE

Under normal circumstances, exercise is widely touted and generates numerous physical and psychological benefits. Much information on the market explains the physiological advantages such as cardiovascular strengthening, lowered blood pressure, reduced pain, increased mental acuity, and euphoric feelings. One might speculate that exercise would do wonders for clients with PTSD.

Much research such as that by Sime (1984) clearly specified that exercise can decrease anxiety and depression. An easy assumption would be to randomly prescribe exercise for PTSD survivors. Another convincing piece of information comes from Westerlund (1992), who worked with incest survivors, and showed that exercise provided a sense of control over their bodies. We know that PTSD survivors desperately need control of physiological, mental, and emotional levels. As with other forms of self-regulation, some clients may benefit, while others may not. In general, exercise is known to reduce anxiety so aerobics or running is a productive method of releasing the ever present tension that PTSD clients experience. Exercise can serve as an outlet for an increased arousal system.

Nevertheless, Jon Allen (1995) reminds us that some clients may find aerobic exercise to be anxiety-provoking. Exercise increases arousal initially and a client could associate the feeling of arousal with the trauma. Allen notes that clients could experience flashbacks, dissociate, become confused and disoriented, and possibly experience a panic attack. Obviously, moderation is the key until the client knows what is helpful and what is not.

Anaerobic exercise can also be employed. An example is weight lifting which uses short bursts of energy, intermittent with rest periods. Some clients have found that trauma-related anxiety symptoms were reduced or released by pushing against a heavy object or lifting weights. Perhaps these movements were symbolic or representative of unconscious material. For instance, a woman who was raped might find relief in thrusting a heavy weight away from her body, symbolizing an ability to push the attacker away. This exercise could assist in a feeling of mastery or control.

Self-styled exercise such as gardening, walking in a park, sightseeing, or any activities that keep the client moving at a leisurely pace can assist in the healing process. Often it is helpful for a client to start slow to check their tolerance. Not all clients are able to exercise, particularly in a vigorous manner.

On a positive note, Allen (1995) states that exercise can, *"provide a sense of predictability, control, and accomplishment. Success is just doing it regularly—at whatever level."*

## BREATHWORK

Breathwork is another popular form of relaxation. Since trauma spectrum clients frequently suffer from increased arousal, it is important for them to gain control and mastery of their body. If breathing exercises are performed correctly, they can assist with anxiety management. However, not everyone can use breathing techniques. For instance, Allen (1995) cautions us that any activity that causes a person to gasp for breath, even though it is unrelated to the trauma, can evoke traumatic memories and cause re-experiencing of the original event. If a client is working hard at accomplishing a particular breathing technique and it brings up memories, obviously another version should be tried and the distressing technique eliminated. This difficulty in relaxation is known as *relaxation-induced anxiety,* and some clients associate relaxation with letting down their guard. In order to be successful, they must be certain they are in a safe place. It is noteworthy that Walter Cannon's fight or flight response, which activates the sympathetic nervous system, is the exact opposite of the state of relaxation which slows metabolism (Allen, 1995). Some clients could feel vulnerable in such a relaxed state. Others might begin to dissociate or feel spacey. Despite the obstacles to relaxing, the following four techniques have been beneficial to numerous traumatized clients. Often these techniques are used for relaxation before processing traumatic material, as well as for closure of the therapy session.

## A. Diaphragmatic Breathing

1. Sit comfortably erect in a chair with feet on the floor. Wear loose clothing which permits ease of breathing.
2. Place hand on diaphragm to ensure proper breathing. (If clients are concerned that they may be experiencing shallow breathing, instruct them to lie on their back. It will naturally force them into diaphragmatic breathing.)
3. Inhale slowly through the nostrils filling the lungs with oxygen. Then exhale slowly through the nostrils. Nostril breathing is preferred, as opposed to breathing through the mouth, because it stimulates important brain centers.
4. Use this technique several times during the day, as needed, for 5 to 10 minutes.

**Note:** You may want to investigate using BIODOT skin thermometers to measure the degree of relaxation that the client is achieving while using breathing techniques. BIODOTs are small, round, black dots with adhesive that you place in the webbed area between the thumb and the forefinger. As you relax, the colors will change from black, which indicates very tense, to other colors, which indicates how relaxed the client is. The chart is as follows: black: very tense, amber: tense, yellow: unsettled, green: involved (normal), turquoise: relaxing, blue: calm and violet: very relaxed. Clients can see the amount of relaxation that they are achieving which gives them comfort and confidence that they can begin to control their hyperaroused state. The telephone number for BIODOTs is: 1-800-272-2340.

## B. Visualization

To enhance the diaphragmatic breathing, a client may add some form of visualization. Clients are free to choose an image that is helpful to them. For instance, as clients inhale, they might choose to visualize puffy white clouds (symbolizing life-giving oxygen) filling the body. As they exhale, they could visualize black smoke (typifying toxins in the body) leaving the system.

**Note:** If the client's trauma involved a fire, then the smoke image could be retraumatizing. This is the reason why it is important for clients to choose their own images.

## C. Balloon Breathing

1. Stand upright with arms relaxed at sides.
2. Breathe deeply through the nostrils, filling the lungs. Hold the breath about 5 seconds while tensing all muscles in the body, particularly the neck, shoulders, and upper arms.
3. Consciously become aware of what tension feels like in your body and where it resides. During grief or trauma, some individuals are not aware of how much tension the body is holding, so this purposeful tensing of the muscles accentuates it and brings it to awareness.
4. After holding the breath about 5 seconds and tensing muscles, release the air suddenly through the mouth. (This resembles popping a balloon.) While suddenly releasing the air, the person should lean forward with their arms and hands swinging loosely, as close to the ground as possible.

   Breathing has an important relationship to trauma and grief. Shallow breathing serves as a negative defense function for *cutting off feeling*. When we repress emotions (hold them in) such as fear, anger, or grief, it hinders and short circuits breathing. *Conscious deep breathing assists in expressing and releasing emotions appropriately.*

## D. Timed Breathing

This is an excellent technique to slow down the breathing process. The increased arousal that trauma clients may experience could cause them to breathe faster than they should. This places them at risk for re-experiencing or dissociation. The therapist may instruct the client in the following simple steps.

1. Therapist asks client to close his eyes.
2. Therapist uses stop watch and asks client to breathe normally and count the breaths sub-vocally.
3. Client inhales and exhales for a minute. Therapist calls the time to stop. (If client breathes 18–22 times a minute, it indicates high anxiety. A relaxed person should breathe 8–12 times a minute.)
4. Client practices counting breaths until he can gain control and lower the number of breaths.

This technique is excellent for physiological control and mastery. The client can then time themselves whenever it is needed. This simple method adds to their repertoire of self-regulation techniques.

## Sensorimotor Psychotherapy

Sensorimotor psychotherapy was developed by Pat Ogden (2000) and is based on her clinical experience. Ogden states that:

> Trauma profoundly affects the body and many symptoms of traumatized individuals are somatically based . . . .Sensorimotor psychotherapy is a method that integrates sensorimotor processing with cognitive and emotional processing in the treatment of trauma . . . by using the body (rather than cognition or emotion) as a primary entry point in processing trauma. Sensorimotor psychotherapy directly treats the effects of trauma on the body which in turn facilitates emotional and cognitive processing.

This process is an excellent supplemental therapy and isn't designed to function alone. Ogden explains, *"The full spectrum of sensorimotor psychotherapy integrates sensorimotor processing with emotional and cognitive processing."*

Ogden cites an example of a woman who had been sexually abused as a child and explains how the therapy would proceed. She asked the client to revisit the trauma and notice the bodily sensations. Since the woman was sexually abused as a child, she begins to re-experience those bodily sensations such as submitting and dissociating from her body, which was evidenced as numbness, muscle flaccidity, and feeling paralyzed. The client simultaneously felt an impulse to fight back which was demonstrated as tension in her jaws and arms. Two different themes were at work and appeared as a *"dissociative split,"* but in therapy, they were easily understood by the client. She was able to recognize that the disintegration wasn't real; in actuality she was experiencing herself as two bodies inside herself expressing two different things. Part of her had to submit and dissociate, and yet another part of her wanted to fight. Understanding this split caused her to heal. It also helped her to accept her dissociation as a way of surviving the horrific abuse.

· As part of this therapy, the client is instructed to move the body in any way that it dictates such as hitting, pushing, kicking, or making a fist. The body has a language of its own which needs to be expressed. These bodily expressions may be performed alone or the client can push against the therapist in a non-violent manner.

Special training is offered in sensorimotor psychotherapy. Clinicians may contact the Sensorimotor Psychotherapy Institute and Naropa University, Boulder, CO. (www.sensorimotorpsychotherapy.org)

## TRAUMA TOUCH THERAPY

Trauma touch therapy is a hands-on body-oriented modality which falls into the broad category of massage therapies. It assists the emotionally numb client to feel again. Since the body remembers the trauma on a cellular level, it is important to work with the somatic memories that it is holding. Clients probably wonder why numbing is considered a problem when it seems quite natural for them to not want to feel their pain. The difficulty lies in the fact that the numbing process can't differentiate which portion of the person should be anesthetized, and which should continue to feel. Happiness, energy, and motivation may also be blocked along with painful memories.

Trauma touch is a slow gentle therapy which integrates the mind and body. Since the body or parts of the body may be temporarily disowned or dissociated, it is essential that they be resurrected and reconnected to the whole. In a conversation with Chris Smith, (1993)the founder of trauma touch therapy, she explained that she is a survivor of sexual abuse and understood the need for healthy touch from the personal and professional level. She developed this approach to work with her clients who had been traumatized by domestic violence, childhood abuse, illness or death of a loved one, or any other traumatic event. It generally consists of 10 sessions and the client is in control of the process. Questions are asked such as: *"In what part of your body do you feel the pain or tension?"* *"Describe the pain or tension."* Then the therapist asks permission to touch it, if it is a location that doesn't violate ethical standards. If granted, the gentle touch massage begins. The client is typically clothed and can sit in a chair or lie on the massage table. Smith doesn't claim that she conducts psychotherapy, although her touch therapy enables emotions to surface. She requires that clients work with a psychotherapist to interpret the meaning of the emotions and doesn't treat clients unless they are in therapy with someone.

Clients tell the trauma touch therapist what is needed. Perhaps they simply hold a spot or they gently massage it; maybe they simply assume a quiet calming stance. The goal is helping the client to view the body as a safe place, and this goal is realized in baby steps. The therapist must be alert to reading the client's body language as to how the touch is affecting them. Slowly but surely, the client is awakened and the numbness disappears, emotions and memories surface, and healing takes place.

## MASSAGE

Massage therapy has become a popular, acceptable stress management technique. The best therapy is performed by a trained massage therapist and requires a certificate through the American Massage Therapy Association. Since a traumatized person may be anxious and in an aroused state, various types of massages may be helpful.

### A. Mechanical Shiatsu

Mechanical shiatsu uses a small machine which serves as a powerful massager that can soothe aches and pains and relieve tension. It is convenient to use at home or during breaks at work. It consists of two circulating balls that provide deep tissue pressure on whatever portion of the body is placed between the rotating balls. This technique may work well with clients who are unable to tolerate touch from another person.

### B. Acupressure/Acupuncture

Acupressure, an ancient Chinese remedy, affirms that energy blockages cause physical, mental, and emotional problems. Many of these problems are relieved by putting pressure on certain locations/points of the body. The pressure points may also be stimulated by acupuncture which uses needles. Some traumatized clients may resist acupuncture, but could benefit from acupressure.

## C. Swedish Massage

Swedish massage, the gentlest, most soothing form of massage, requires the trained hands of a massage therapist. Soft lights, scented candles, soothing music, and creamy oils and lotions often accompany the massage. Since traumatized clients frequently experience anxiety and tension, a massage can refresh and relax them for a short period of time before they return to the difficult adjustments they are making in their lives. It is important to remember that massage reduces the stress hormone cortisol and releases the mood-building serotonin.

**Note:** Not every client will benefit from massage. Clients such as those who are rape victims or who were physically or sexually abused may be retraumatized by being touched. As with any therapy, it is person-specific and relative to the needs of the client.

## MEDITATION

Since recovery from PTSD uses multiple modes of treatments, the basic self-care treatment of meditation has its place in the healing process. Regaining some amount of control over the physiological arousal in the body is paramount and meditation assists with that goal. Meditation is defined as a relaxation technique that increases one's ability to focus or concentrate. It assists in producing a calm, relaxed mind. Herbert Benson (1975) recommends four elements that are required for relaxation and a meditative process:

1. A quiet environment without distractions and disturbances
2. A mental device as a focal point such as a visual image or sound
3. A passive, calm attitude
4. A comfortable relaxed body position

In trauma, the client may be experiencing the interruptions of intrusive thoughts and images. *"Exclusive meditation,"* a technique that calms and quiets the mind, assists clients by blocking distracting thoughts, and teaches them to focus on one single object. The client may want to practice concentrating on an image such as a bowl of fruit, a vase of summer flowers, a loved one's face, a glass of ice water, a beautiful mountain scene, a cascading waterfall, or any other image that evokes a peaceful picture. If disturbing thoughts enter, the client can choose to let them pass and exit. The client is instructed to keep the focus on the desired object, holding it as the principal focus of concentration. Clients need to grasp the concept that *"thinking is stressing."* Therefore any reprieve from thinking of the trauma gives clients some sense of control over intrusive thoughts and images.

St. Francis of Assisi explained that distracting thoughts are like birds flying in the air. You can't stop them from their flight, but they don't have to make a nest in your hair. In like manner, you can't stop distracting thoughts from passing by, but you don't have to focus on them.

A technique called *"thought stopping"* is a simple form of meditation. For five or ten minutes, a person can concentrate on a continuous sound such as an air conditioner, heater, a bubbling fish tank, or the client's own breathing. Every time the person drifts into thinking, then a conscious shift must be made to listen, and focus again only on the sound. At first, a traumatized person may only be able to meditate in this manner for a few seconds, but as they practice it, they will be able to *stop their thoughts* for longer periods of time. With the constant bombardment of thoughts during the aftermath of a traumatic experience, a little rest can be deeply appreciated.

## MINDFULNESS

Mindfulness falls under the general category of meditation. This technique uses all the senses in focusing and concentrating exclusively on the activity that one is involved in at the moment. The person is totally present and available to the activity, which could be anything the person is doing; examining the colors and shape of a flower, preparing a dessert, mowing the lawn, or petting a cat.

Why is the practice of mindfulness helpful with a traumatized person? Because mindfulness is the opposite of dissociation and it provides some sense of control in keeping the client in the present. Very little literature exists regarding effective ways to deal with dissociation; however, this technique can assist on certain occasions. For instance, the client could choose some object before processing traumatic material in a counseling session and the object could be called upon if the client begins to dissociate. The client may choose to focus on a picture in the room, which represents the here and now. Perhaps the client chooses to focus on the flower arrangement on the therapist's desk. If the client dissociates momentarily, a gentle reminder from the therapist such as, *"focus on the different colors in the flower arrangement"* could change the direction of the client's movement and attention.

Dissociation is linked with a sense of non-reality; even the harmless habit of daydreaming can be a mild form of temporary dissociation. Mindfulness keeps us in the here and now by focusing on what we are experiencing in the present, whether that is the simple act of breathing or listening to the hum of the air conditioner. The benefit of this form of therapy lies in its ability to separate the past from the present. As human beings we can truly only live in the present.

## NUTRITIONAL SUPPLEMENTATION

Traumatic stress is a major stressor, and as such it quickly depletes a victim's body of certain vitamins, minerals, and other essential nutrients. I would like to introduce a prestigious doctor who many of you may want to contact with regard to his expertise or the various health products that he himself has developed.

Dr. Doug Hansen, MD earned his medical degree with honors at the University of Illinois College of Medicine and completed his residency training at St. Anthony Hospital in Denver, Colorado. Dr. Hansen is a triple board-certified family physician, clinical lipidologist, and nutrition specialist. Dr. Hansen has been practicing in Denver since 1999 and, in addition to his clinical practice, serves as professor of medicine at the University Of Colorado School Of Medicine.

Dr. Hansen is a nationally-featured speaker focusing on heart disease, hypertension, cholesterol, diabetes, and nutrition. He has been featured on NBC's Today Show and MSNBC and has contributed to many books and publications including *Breakthroughs in Natural Healing 2012* and *Building Foundations for Change* from the bestselling *"Wake Up and Live the Life You Love"* Series.

Dr. Hansen is proud to be distinguished as a Patients' Choice Award winner, an honor bestowed to the top 5% of physicians in the United States as voted by patients for the past consecutive 4 years. Additionally, Dr. Hansen was one of the select few physicians recently honored with the prestigious *Compassionate Doctor Certification*. Only those physicians with near perfect overall bedside manner scores, as voted by their patients, are selected for the Compassionate Doctor recognition. Of the nation's 720,000 active physicians, only 3% were accorded this honor.

The following information was graciously contributed by Dr. Hansen. *See Dr. Schupp's note regarding supplements and contact information.*

## AN UPDATE ON NUTRITIONAL SUPPLEMENTATION FOR THE PREVENTION AND TREATMENT OF PTSD

While psychotherapy and medications form the cornerstone of PTSD management, natural therapies for the prevention and treatment of PTSD are becoming increasingly prevalent. Unfortunately, current research regarding the use of natural therapies for PTSD is sparse. The majority of natural supplements for the treatment of PTSD are used based on experiential or anecdotal evidence. As such, the use of nutritional supplements in PTSD should be primarily to augment conventional therapies and only under the direct supervision of a physician.

Proposed nutritional therapeutic options include:

- **Multivitamins:** Researchers have shown a link between nutritional deficiencies and psychiatric disorders from major depression to psychosis. This data suggests both the benefit of a well balanced diet as well as the potential for vitamin and mineral supplementation.

  The dietary intake pattern of the population in America and Asia frequently reflects a clinical or subclinical deficiency in many nutrients including essential vitamins and minerals. The degree of psychological impairment frequently correlates with the severity of deficiency in these nutrients, but can be difficult to ascertain through clinical testing. Studies have suggested that the nutritional supplementation may be effective in reducing psychological symptoms.

  A good multivitamin supplement should contain at minimum the antioxidant vitamins A, C, D, E, and the Bs, as well as certain trace minerals according to the FDA guidelines.

- **Omega-3 Fatty Acids:** Several small studies have shown that Omega 3 fatty acids, such as those found in fish oil and krill oil, may be useful in the prevention and/or symptom reduction of depression, traumatic brain injury, attention deficit disorder, and PTSD especially when taken before or immediately after trauma.

  A recent Japanese study examined the correlation between blood levels of essential omega-3 and omega-6 fatty acids and the risk of accident-related PTSD (Matsuoka et al., 2013). The study measured serum fatty acid levels in patients severely injured in auto accidents, and divided the patients into 3 groups based on these levels. Six months after their auto accident, those with the highest blood levels of omega-3 EPA or omega-6 AA were significantly less likely to show signs of PTSD.

  Compared to the participants with the lowest blood levels of omega-3 EPA and omega-6 AA, the risk for PTSD was significantly lower among those with blood levels ranking in the middle or high categories. The results were adjusted to account for the known effects of age, sex, alcohol habits, smoking habits, and education level on vulnerability to post-crash PTSD. The finding that higher levels of omega-3 EPA may reduce

PTSD risk is remarkably similar to the link found in a meta-analysis of studies on depression and EPA (Lin et al., 2011). Prospective data looking at the inverse correlation between omega-3 supplementation and anxiety shows benefits starting at doses of 2 grams of daily EPA equivalent supplementation.

- **SAMe:** In small studies, S-adenosy-L-methionine has shown superiority to placebo in treating depressive disorder. The beneficial effect of SAMe is theorized to be due to neurotransmitter enhancement, and can begin within a few days of initiation. SAMe should be used with caution as a few case reports of mania have been described with its use. Typical doses of SAMe are between 200 and 1600 milligrams daily.
- **Theanine:** L-theanine, an amino acid found in tea leaves, has been reported to promote a calming effect. Typical doses of L-theanine range between 10 and 20 milligrams daily.
- **Melatonin:** Melatonin, when taken before bed, may be helpful to support sleep and immune function. Typical doses of Melatonin range between 0.5 and 6 milligrams nightly. Melatonin is often taken in combination with L-theanine as indicated above.
- **Kava:** Kava has been shown somewhat useful in helping with the symptoms of stress and anxiety. Kava should be used with extreme caution as it may aggravate depression, interacts with several pharmaceutical medications, and in rare cases has caused liver damage.

---

**Dr. Schupp's note:**

Dr. Hansen has produced a physician engineered supplement line, a few of which are listed here. One product called Thrivetality Chocolate Meal Replacement Shake is an excellent choice for a patient suffering with PTSD in that they are often unable to eat. Considering the interaction between nutritional deficiencies and mental disease, his multi-vitamin named Thrivetality ONE would ensure that those basics are met. When considering the recent Japanese study and its research on the importance of fish oil, it's helpful to know that Dr. Hansen had already developed a fish oil supplement named Thrivetality Ultra Meg. For more information, call 303-730-2167 or visit website www.AltitudeMedicine.com.

## PSYCHOPHARMACOLOGY

Davidson and van der Kolk (1996) reviewed the psychopharmacological treatment for PTSD and came up with the following goals for the use of various medications for PTSD.*

1. Reduction of frequency and/or severity of intrusive symptoms
2. Reduction in the tendency to interpret incoming stimuli as recurrences of the trauma
3. Reduction in conditioned hyperarousal to stimuli reminiscent of the trauma, as well as in generalized hyperarousal
4. Reduction in avoidance behavior
5. Improvement in depressed mood and numbing
6. Reduction in psychotic or dissociative symptoms
7. Reduction of impulsive aggression against self and others

If a medication doesn't serve these purposes, then the need for it should be re-evaluated. These goals still provide current guidance for the use of medication.

Many medical and psychological professionals are claiming that selective serotonin reuptake inhibitors (SSRIs), such as paroxetine (Paxil), sertraline (Zoloft), fluvoxamine (Luvox), fluoxetine (Prozac), and citalopram (Celexa), are the treatment of choice for PTSD and other trauma-related disorders and conditions. Although not everyone agrees, one hypothesis for a biological basis for PTSD, as well as depression, would be a deficiency of the neurotransmitter serotonin. The benefits of SSRIs have been clearly observed in clinical practice, and this class of drugs has outperformed other types in drug trials. SSRIs have proven to assist with such PTSD symptoms as intrusive recollections, avoidance, numbing, hyperarousal, negative alterations in cognitions and mood. It also treats comorbid disorders such as obsessive-compulsive disorder, major depressive disorder, panic disorder, and alcohol abuse. Research by Friedman (1990) and Brady, et al. (1995) have shown that SSRIs are also helpful in regulating PTSD symptoms such as rage, impulsivity, obsessional thinking, and suicidal ideation. The SSRIs' beneficial effect is due to their ability to block the presynaptic reuptake of serotonin which leaves

---

*Reprinted with permission from Guilford Publications, New York. Traumatic Stress, Bessel van der Kolk, 1996.

more serotonin within the system. It is believed by many experts that SSRI medications can actually reverse the negative impact that traumatic stress has on the brain. For instance, the work of Bremner (2002) has proven that atrophy occurs in the hippocampus due to increased cortisol. Gould, et al. (1998) found that the hippocampus was capable of *"neurogenesis,"* which means that even in adulthood, new neurons could grow. Serotonin assisted with the reproduction of new brain cells.

Bessel van der Kolk, et al. (1994) found that fluoxetine, commonly known as Prozac, when administered at doses of 40 mg. or higher was beneficial in civilian-related PTSD, but not combat-related PTSD. Later studies (2012) have confirmed these findings. The effectiveness of the medication varies depending on the origins of the PTSD. Brady, et al. (2000) have demonstrated that sertraline (Zoloft) was quite effective in treating women with PTSD, with only moderate improvement in men. Gender, then, also affects the performance of the drug.

In addition to gender, age plays a role in regard to the performance of a drug. DeBoer, et al. (1992) has discovered that selective serotonin reuptake inhibitor antidepressants frequently provide better results than benzodiazepine hypnotics when treating symptoms of disturbed sleep and dreaming in elderly trauma victims.

Not all clients can take SSRIs and some might benefit from carefully managed benzodiazepines such as alprazolam (Xanax) and clonazepam (Klonopin). These anti-anxiety drugs can reduce anxiety, fear, insomnia, hyperarousal, jumpiness, anger, startle response, and irritability. Resick (2001) states that clonidine (Catapres) and propranolol (Inderal), seem to assist in curbing sympathetic arousal and adrenergic activity. According to Kinzie and Leung (1989), Kolb, Burris, and Griffiths (1984), and Perry (1994), these drugs reduce nightmares, intrusive memories, hypervigilance, startle responses, insomnia, and angry outbursts. Southwick, et al. (1994) have studied the effects of tricyclic antidepressants and monoamine oxidase inhibitors (MAOI) on PTSD clients and found that they were somewhat effective for re-experiencing symptoms, but not for avoidance and arousal.

Most clinicians today wouldn't diagnose PTSD clients as having a psychotic disorder. If clients experience dissociation, it is linked only to the trauma, not randomly across the board as in a psychotic state. Most of the PTSD symptoms such as agitation, paranoia, impulsivity, dissociation, and hypervigilance can be mitigated by either antidepressants or anti-adrenergic medications. It would only be the occasional client who would require an anti-psychotic drug. Some psychiatrists believe that medications such as risperidone (Risperdal), quetiapine (Seroquel), and olanzapine (Zyprexa) could be considered, but should be administered sparingly.

Foa, et al. (1999) have shown that a panel of experts recommended SSRIs as the best available treatment of that time. The same group of experts also felt that combination therapies with mood stabilizing agents should be administered. Probably the most important decision regarding the efficacy of SSRIs in the treatment of PTSD was the decision by the U.S. Food and Drug Administration to put their stamp of approval on sertraline as a drug to treat PTSD. Sertraline, commonly known as Zoloft, reduced symptoms in all three areas of intrusion, hyperarousal and avoidance/numbing. With the new DSM-5, we have a fourth category which is alterations in negative cognitions and moods which responds to SSRIs as well. The U.S. Food and Drug Administration based its decision on two large trials conducted by Brady, et al. (2000) and Davidson, Malik, and Sutherland (1996) where participants received either a placebo or sertraline. Prior to these studies, some researchers seriously wondered if PTSD sufferers would have to take separate drugs for the PTSD symptoms. Therefore, it is good news that sertraline, as well as other SSRIs, treats all four clusters.

## CURRENT PSYCHOPHARMACOLOGICAL STUDIES FOR PTSD

The Agency for Healthcare Research and Quality was contracted by the U.S. Department of Health and Human Services, and conducted a study on June 6, 2012 which brings us interesting information concerning interventions for PTSD. They reviewed various studies on medications and their efficacy in preventing PTSD. Medications studied were as follows:

**Pharmacological Treatments for Adults With Posttraumatic Stress Disorder (PTSD)**

| Pharmacological Agent(s) | Medications |
|---|---|
| Selective serotonin-reuptake inhibitors | citalopram, escitalopram, fluoxetine, fluvoxamine, paroxetine, and sertraline |
| Serotonin and norepinephrine reuptake inhibitors | duloxetine, desvenlafaxine, and venlafaxine |
| Other second-generation antidepressants | bupropion, mirtazapine, nefazodone, and trazodone |
| Tricyclic antidepressants | imipramine, amitriptyline, and desipramine |

| Monoamine oxidase inhibitors | phenelzine, isocarboxazid, selegiline, and tranylcypromine |
|---|---|
| Alpha-blockers | prazosin |
| Beta-blockers | propranolol |
| Benzodiazepines | alprazolam, diazepam, lorazepam, and clonazepam |
| Anticonvulsants | topiramate, tiagabine, lamotrigine, carbamazepine, divalproex, and gabapentin |
| Non-benzodiazepine sedatives/hypnotics | zolpidem, eszopiclone, rozerem, and zaleplon |
| Second-generation (atypical) antipsychotics | olanzapine and risperidone |
| Narcotic medication | morphine |
| Steroids | hydrocortisone |
| Opioid antagonists | naltrexone |

Drugs such as propranolol, morphine, glucocorticoids, and selective serotonin reuptake inhibitors were carefully critiqued and reviewed.

***Selective Serotonin Reuptake Inhibitors—SSRIs:*** Their conclusion based on all the studies they reviewed was that SSRI antidepressants are the drugs most frequently prescribed. They are modestly effective for civilian trauma-related PTSD but no more effective than a placebo when administered to military veterans. The SSRIs may diminish the more severe clinical problems after trauma. This result is possibly due to nonspecific effects on other monoamines or through neuroprotective effects in the brain or through increases in neurotrophic factors that block the down-regulation of brain-derived neurotrophic factors. Since the DSM-5 adds a fourth cluster of negative cognitions and moods, we can probably anticipate that SSRIs will cover most or all of that area.

***Propranolol:*** This beta-adrenergic antagonist has been of interest in several studies as a *preventive* treatment for PTSD. There have been mixed results with this drug and controversy regarding its use continues to cause debate. In some successful studies it prevented the imprint of the trauma on the brain. In other words, it has the ability to attenuate the emotional response and memory of the trauma. It decreases the emotional memory and episodic memory for the event, which causes ethical concerns about long term implications of emotional and episodic memories. Despite its known abilities, the NIH group (2012) stated that propranolol failed to show any clear benefit, when compared to placebo, in reducing physiological reactivity during traumatic imagery, severity of PTSD, or the rate of the PTSD diagnostic outcome. Other individuals have continued to test it and believe it has a place with combat veterans and others who develop severe PTSD.

Interestingly enough, ClinicalTrials.gov, a service of the National Institutes of Health (2013) began a multisite clinical efficacy study starting November 2012 and ending November 2015. As of November 2013 one report indicated the University Hospital, Toulouse, France was still recruiting participants. It seems that at present these studies are occurring in several locations in France. The purpose of the study is to test propranolol, when given during a re-evocation of a traumatic memory to ascertain if it is capable of reducing subsequent PTSD symptoms associated with that memory. For further information contact University Hospital, Toulouse, ClinicalTrials.gov. identifier. Hopefully further research will clarify its efficacy and perhaps its appropriate population.

**Morphine:** This opiate analgesic has prevented PTSD in persons experiencing physical injury from a traumatic event. The patients who were prescribed higher doses of morphine had a lower incidence of PTSD after a 3-month follow-up. Combat injured military personnel in Iraq were administered morphine during early trauma care and they had a significantly lower risk of PTSD diagnosis. Perhaps *"the more pain, the more risk for PTSD"* would apply here. This study points to the importance of pain control in physically injured persons. However, the role of opiates after severe psychological trauma remains unclear.

**Cortisol:** This naturally occurring stress hormone released from the adrenal glands when the hypothalamic pituitary adrenal (HPA) axis is activated during a trauma. (See the Response to Trauma Diagram in Chapter One.) Since traumatized people may have depleted their cortisol, it is observed that many of them exhibit low cortisol levels after a trauma. This finding has led to the hypothesis that exogenous administration of cortisol may prevent HPA axis dysregulation, thus hindering the development of PTSD.

**Glucocorticoids:** Glucocorticoids were administered to individuals either during or immediately after the trauma. It was found that they were significantly less vulnerable to developing PTSD as compared to people who didn't receive the glucocorticoids. Unfortunately, some factors could not be controlled due to the naturalistic settings in which the studies took place. For example, other medications and treatment procedures could not be controlled. Therefore results are not as clear as we'd like.

A Comparative Effectiveness Review No. 92 (2013) prepared by the Agency for Healthcare Research and Quality for the U.S. Department of Health and Human Services gives us additional, current information regarding medications. Many pharmacological therapies have been studied for treatment of patients with PTSD, including selective serotonin reuptake inhibitors (SSRIs), serotonin and norepinephrine reuptake inhibitors (SNRIs), other second-generation antidepressants, tricyclic antidepressants, monoamine oxidase (MAO) inhibitors, alpha-blockers, second-generation (atypical) antipsychotics, anticonvulsants (mood stabilizers), and benzodiazepines. Currently, only paroxetine and sertraline are approved by the U.S. Food and Drug Administration for treatment of patients with PTSD.

However, most guidelines identify trauma-focused psychological treatments over pharmacological treatments as a preferred first step and view medications as an adjunct or a next-line treatment. Among pharmacological treatments, they found evidence of moderate strength supporting the efficacy of fluoxetine, paroxetine, sertraline, topiramate, and venlafaxine for improving PTSD symptoms. Risperidone may also have some benefit for reduction of PTSD symptoms. Paroxetine and venlafaxine also had evidence of efficacy for inducing remission.

The Comparative Effectiveness Review No. 92 (2013) also contained evidence supporting the efficacy of fluoxetine (Prozac) for improving anxiety symptoms, and that of venlafaxine (Effexor) for improving quality of life and of venlafaxine (Effexor) and paroxetine (Paxil) for improving functional impairment for adults with PTSD. The review found just one trial meeting inclusion criteria that directly compared a psychological treatment with a pharmacological treatment. It compared eye movement desensitization reprocessing therapy (EMDR), fluoxetine (Prozac), and placebo. The trial found that EMDR- and (Prozac) fluoxetine-treated subjects had similar improvements in PTSD symptoms, rates of remission, and loss of PTSD diagnosis at the end of treatment. At 6-month follow-up, those treated with EMDR had higher remission rates and greater reductions in depression symptoms than those who received only fluoxetine (Prozac). They concluded that the head-to-head evidence was insufficient to draw any firm conclusions about comparative effectiveness, primarily due to unknown consistency (with data from just one study) and lack of precision.

In addition, paroxetine (Paxil) has evidence supporting its efficacy for improving depression symptoms and functional impairment and venlafaxine (Effexor) has evidence supporting its efficacy for improving depression symptoms, quality of life, and functional impairment. Further, the network meta-analysis found paroxetine (Paxil) to be one of the best treatments.

For many of the treatments, studies did not include any follow-up after completion of treatment to assess whether benefits were maintained. This was particularly true for the pharmacological treatments because trials generally reported outcomes after 8 to 12 weeks of treatment. In addition, pharmaceutical companies funded the majority of trials assessing medications.

Regardless of the 2013 study, it is up to each medical doctor, psychiatrist, physician's assistant and any other prescribing health care professional to make their own decision as to what will be best for their patients. Some health care professionals are advocating different forms of psychotherapy first and using medications as a second choice. The field of psychopharmacology is constantly changing and we are treating trauma with many new and innovative treatments.

# CHAPTER FIVE

# TREATMENT TECHNIQUES FOR TRAUMA

## THE RELATIONSHIP AS THERAPY

Trauma survivors have experienced the world as an unsafe place due to unexpected events that have been out of their control. Some have also encountered or lived with people who violated their trust and perpetrated harm against them. Because of their perceived lack of control and misused, misplaced trust, clients may be rightfully suspicious of baring their souls to a stranger that claims to "help and care." Because of the fragility of clients' emotions, shattering and retraumatization could easily occur. Counselors must proceed with caution like a skilled surgeon who delicately and deftly uses the correct instrument with accuracy and precision.

With trauma clients, the relationship itself becomes the initial tool. Compassion must be conveyed before competence can be appreciated. Trust must be built and established before facilitation can occur. Until trust is built to some degree, testing for posttraumatic stress disorder or other related traumas may need to be delayed or perhaps eliminated altogether. Since PTSD and trauma-based conditions are easy to diagnose in an informal way, to administer a test to a traumatized client may appear harsh and abrasive. Counselors need to be a person first, professional second.

Every human being has a deep longing and need to be heard and understood. Of all clients, trauma survivors need these elements more than most. Even though the counselor may not have experienced any situation that remotely resembles the trauma of the client, the counselor can use bonding techniques such as Identity Clues. Every client possesses certain traits, mannerisms, characteristics, beliefs, and behaviors that constitute the individuality of that person. The more similar counselors appear to clients, the greater comfort the client will experience. *"Commonalities create comfort;*

*differences produce distance"* (Schupp, 2003). If clients are comfortable, they are more likely to discuss the trauma. If they are afraid the counselor can't handle the pain of their experience, then they may not talk about it. Therefore, it is extremely important to use rapport-building techniques such as the following.

Since Alan Schore (2007), Stephen Porges (2012), R. Scaer (2005), and Janina Fisher (2010) emphasize our attachment and affect with our clients, both conscious and unconscious, it behooves us to communicate with our bodies, facial expressions, eyes, tonal quality, emotions, and words. The following techniques are a combination of in-depth bonding and connecting with our clients by using conscious left hemispheric techniques and unconscious right hemispheric techniques.

## IDENTITY CLUES

1. Agree when possible
2. Paraphrase or restate their words, experiences, ideas, beliefs, values, feelings, principles
3. Match their verbal energy
4. Imitate some of client's body language

Linda J. Schupp, 2003

The technique of agreement can support the client by providing some commonality and similarities, as well as comfort and connection.

Jennifer is the wife of John who worked as a pilot for a large airline. Unfortunately, his plane crashed in a thunderstorm killing him and many passengers. Jennifer came for counseling and, in addition to her intense grief, she complained about jumpiness and anxiety. Although she didn't recognize it, she was experiencing the startle response which is common in PTSD. Jennifer told her therapist:

> *"Every time I hear a truck roaring down the highway, I relive my perception of John's death."*

The therapist may choose to respond:

> *"I probably would react just like you if I had been through the same experience."*

This statement agrees with the client in a supportive manner, and also validates the normalcy of her reactions. Jennifer's faith has been radically shaken and she poses an unanswerable question to the therapist.

*"I prayed to God everyday asking him to protect my husband in his flights as a pilot. Why didn't God answer my prayers?"*

The counselor, in this case, shares the same faith as Jennifer and responds

*"You know, Jennifer, I also pray for protection of my loved ones, and I would be asking the same question if my husband had died in an accident."*

The technique of agreement supports the client's feelings and questioning, thus providing an open door for Jennifer to discuss and evaluate her theological beliefs. Trauma deeply touches the spiritual components of the fabric of life and can shatter one's faith at a time when it is most needed. As counselors, we can facilitate the feelings, frustration, questions, and pondering. One of the healing components in trauma is to assist our clients in learning how to live without answers. Those who provide pat answers to the unspeakable horrors that some of our clients experience inflict further damage on that suffering population. Therapists may choose to simply agree in an honest forthright manner whenever possible.

The popular technique of paraphrasing has been titled in many ways such as reflective listening, pacing, mirroring, backtracking, and restating. Whatever label it wears, paraphrasing is the only technique that provides "proof positive" that we have truly entered the trauma survivor's world of perception. It may meet some of their most intense therapeutic needs.

To express the inexpressible, to speak the unspeakable, and to know that one has been heard, understood, and validated, is a gift and service that perhaps only a caring counselor can provide. There are numerous reasons for a counselor to paraphrase; however, some are more relevant than others for trauma survivors.

### The Need to Paraphrase

1. Meets client's deepest needs to be heard and understood
2. Reveals that counselors are not afraid of client's pain
3. Encourages clients to express more fully and to continue sharing
4. Conveys that counselors are connected to clients in their journey
5. Proves that counselors can handle whatever horrific situations clients need to share

This technique can also provide counselors with a non-hasty response when they don't know what to say or they need to momentarily regroup.

Let's look at how paraphrasing can meet some of Jennifer's needs in the counseling session. Jennifer is continuing to relive the traumatic untimely death of her husband and expressing thoughts about what John experienced before the airplane crashed.

> *"How horrible for John when he realized he was going to die. He couldn't protect himself or his passengers. What agony he must have experienced. Perhaps he wondered how his death might affect me and our baby girl."*

The counselor could respond with the following paraphrase.

> *"It must be difficult for you, Jennifer, when you try to figure out what John was thinking, feeling, and experiencing before his death. I'm sure you wonder what his thoughts were in regard to you and the baby. That must have been agonizing for him at that time and it is certainly painful for you at this time."*

Paraphrasing in this example captures the essence of what Jennifer is stating, believing, pondering, and feeling and then reflects it in the counselor's own words. With some originality on the counselor's part, it doesn't sound like Polly parroting. If the counselor feels that a paraphrase might sound patronizing, then a qualifier could be offered prior to the paraphrase.

> *"Jennifer, I know how painful it is for you to think about and express your thoughts surrounding the moments before John died, and because our discussion is relevant to your healing, I want to be certain I'm following your thoughts and feelings. If I heard you correctly . . ."*

If a counselor uses paraphrasing, the client recognizes that the counselor has walked into her trauma, heard her pain, and understood the situation to the degree possible. If there was ever a time to use paraphrasing, it is with a traumatized client who has allowed a clinician to see inside the gaping wounds of the soul. Counselors can reflect with accuracy, care, and concern that the client has been heard on the deepest level.

Imitating the tone and tempo of the client's voice is another bonding technique that wields an unconscious influence. It is a way of matching their verbal energy. Most traumatized, grieving, or ill clients have very little energy in their voices and they may speak slowly and softly. If so, the counselor can slow her pace and tone to more closely, but not exactly, resemble the client's. The counselor should not imitate the client exactly or the client might perceive it as mockery. If the counselor speaks rapidly or loudly when the client is speaking slowly and softly, then the counselor will appear as a complete opposite and become an irritant. Opposition produces stress and strain in the relationship. Similarities and commonalities help the client relax in the counselor's presence. If the traumatized client picks up the pace and speaks in a more animated fashion, the counselor may speed up also and use more expression.

However, a word of warning is due when imitating the tone and tempo. Do not ever imitate negativity. If a traumatized client suddenly screams at the counselor, the counselor shouldn't return the angry response. Anger only escalates anger. In a case of an angry client, a reflective technique could be used such as: *"If I were in your shoes, I might feel the way you do."* Legitimize the behavior as much as possible. Keep in mind, we don't know exactly how we would feel or act until faced with a similar trauma.

Therapists can also enter the world of the client by using body language, since it encompasses 55% of the way messages are sent. It is a powerful signal which can create feelings of connectedness. Therapists can choose to imitate some of the client's body language. All current research validates the importance of this type of unconscious bonding.

If the client is intently leaning toward the counselor, the counselor might lean slightly forward to indicate interest in what is being said. If a client leans backward against the couch, the counselor might wait a few moments, and then lean slightly backward without the counselor's body touching the couch. Counselors don't want to look exactly like the client. The intent is to partially imitate. As with tone of voice, if a counselor imitates the client precisely, or makes a change as soon as he does, it could appear as mockery or patronizing. We don't want the imitation to be obvious. The purpose of the technique is to achieve harmony with the client on an unconscious level.

Mirroring facial expressions can also be useful. If the client appears sad, and is expressing a downcast look, the counselor certainly doesn't want to reflect happiness and joy. Reflect the client's pain with a serious expression. If a traumatized woman, for instance, begins to smile slightly, you might offer a similar smile. This should not be done in a robot-like fashion, but in a natural way, that allows the counselor to become part of the experience bodily. Mirroring the breathing patterns of the client can also be useful, particularly if the therapist wants to decelerate the breathing of the traumatized client. The therapist can join the client, then guide the client into a slower breathing pattern. The more of these bonding techniques that are used, the more comfort the client experiences and the easier it will be to facilitate the healing process.

## Cognitive Behavioral Therapy (CBT)

Aaron Beck, M.D. is recognized as the father of cognitive therapy (1976). Cognitive therapy is a short-term form of psychotherapy based on the concept that the way we think about things affects how we feel. Cognitive therapy is sometimes called cognitive behavior therapy because it aims to help people in the ways they think (the cognitive) and in the ways they act (the behavior). Albert Ellis (1962) is also considered a father of cognitive-behavioral therapy and founder of rational emotive behavior therapy (REBT). Many studies point to the success of these therapies in working with depression, posttraumatic stress disorder, and other trauma-related syndromes. It is a highly regarded treatment for PTSD, and some believe it to be the best treatment that is recorded in the current published literature. There are numerous cognitive behavioral techniques which are used separately and in conjunction with each other. Some of the most frequently used techniques are stress inoculation training (SIT), cognitive processing therapy (CPT), cognitive therapy, exposure therapy, and systematic desensitization. CBT's earlier roots were based in behavior therapy and relearning procedures.

The theory behind CBT draws from the research on learning and conditioning. This theory applies quite naturally to PTSD where clients cognitively recognize and emotionally respond to a life-threatening situation. The client has learned that a particular situation can be dangerous, and the aroused emotions now alert him or her to other potentially threatening circumstances. The client is conditioned to respond to certain emotional stimuli which then create the appropriate needed behaviors.

The following adaptive model by Dr. Linda J. Schupp may be helpful in minimizing the painful emotions that result from distorted thinking surrounding a trauma. The premise of this therapeutic model states that *"we can change our feelings by changing our beliefs."*

**A. Action**

Describe what happened.

**B. Beliefs**

List the negative messages you are repeating to yourself.

1.

2.

3.

## C. Consequences

What emotions are you experiencing regarding the traumatic event?

I feel _____

## D. Defense Attorney

Write out your defense against the negative beliefs in B.

1.

2.

3.

Marjorie and Frank were excited that their daughter Patricia was graduating from college and marrying her fiancé Scott. Patricia never seemed happier and her life's dreams were being fulfilled. Marjorie and Frank decided to buy her a new car to celebrate these landmarks in life. They also figured that Patty and Scott would have a safe enjoyable vehicle to drive on their honeymoon trip. The wedding was lovely, and after the reception, the young couple began their 200 mile trip to a lovely mountain resort. While traveling in the mountains, they came upon an area of slippery roads caused by a downpour of rain. The car hydroplaned, sped uncontrollably off the road, slid over the side of the mountain, killing them both. The parents both experienced intense grief and trauma as would be expected. However, Frank's pain was deepened even further by distorted thoughts connected to the trauma. The use of the following model assisted Frank in eliminating the painful emotions connected to his distorted thinking.

## A. Action

Describe what happened.

*My daughter was killed in a car accident.*

## B. Beliefs

List negative messages you are repeating to yourself.

**1.** *I am responsible for my daughter's death.*
**2.** *I should have bought airplane tickets for them.*

**3.** *I should have bought a better car for them.*

## C. Consequences

What emotions are you experiencing regarding the traumatic event?

*I feel guilty, devastated, and depressed.*

**Note:** These emotions will assist in diagnosing the severity of the impact of the trauma.

## D. Defense Attorney

Write out your defenses against the negative beliefs in B.

**Note:** The following No. 1, 2, and 3 refute the corresponding numbers 1, 2, and 3 of the Beliefs.

**1.** *I'm not a mind reader. There's no way I could have known about or prevented this accident.*

**2.** *They didn't want to fly, because they wanted to sightsee along the way.*

**3.** *They would have driven an older car with more wear on the tires, if I had not bought the new one.*

**Note:** When the negative distorted message appears, the client needs to read and re-read the Defense Attorney (DA). Clinicians may request that clients review the facts of the DA a few minutes in the morning, several times during the day and in the evening before retiring. This repetition bombards the distorted thinking and eventually overpowers it. This technique will assist in minimizing the pain of unwarranted emotions.

## NON-VERBAL TRAUMA THERAPIES

### Art Therapy

Some pain lies so deep within the unconscious recesses of a traumatized client that words are unable to verbalize it. Art therapy is a multimodal approach that provides clients non-verbal emotional expression which may extract traumatic material that would remain unprocessed. Clients may use such techniques as drawing, painting, sculpting, or molding. Colors, texture, patterns, or movements facilitate with a language of their own.

Bernie Siegel (1986), an oncological surgeon uses art therapy with his cancer patients. His intake interview consists of handing out sheets of white paper and crayons, and asking the patients to draw themselves as they perceive their state of health or illness. Siegel believes the drawings are a better indicator regarding the prognosis of the cancer than other diagnostic instruments. Clinicians may consider asking trauma clients to draw themselves in regard to their mental and emotional health. For some clients without adequate words to express the trauma, this tool could prove useful.

Art forms can be especially helpful with children, particularly younger children who lack verbal skills and vocabulary. They may be asked to draw their feelings, and often deeply repressed emotions can surface on paper, canvas, or clay. Talent is not required and anyone can use art therapy.

Art therapy has been successful in treating PTSD patients who have survived the horror and bloodshed of war. Many soldiers were emotionally distraught by memories of destruction and death when they returned home, yet some didn't want to share their experiences verbally. They found expression for the often inexpressible in art therapy.

### Journaling

Journaling opens the door to the conscious and unconscious. It facilitates a healthy expression of perceptions, emotions, reflections, thoughts, conflicts, beliefs, challenges, disappointments, failures, and hopes for the future. Journaling is usually a daily process which keeps a current record of the trauma consequences, emotions, and healing. Because of the frequency of writing, it is easy to track the progress of healing. A backward glance at previous days, weeks, and months compares the past with the present. Trauma victims need encouragement and signposts that are indicative of their progress, so journaling accomplishes that purpose as well as providing self-awareness.

### Writing

Writing can take a variety of forms and is another non-verbal expression which puts words to feelings. Letters can be written to a perpetrator, a deceased loved one, to God or anyone who captivates the myriad of emotions that require release or closure. Letters can express what a person never said or couldn't say, such as apologies, anger, fear, forgiveness, *"I love you"* or *"I hate you."* Many varying, and sometimes conflicting, emotions need to be facilitated. On occasion, it can be a healthy venture to take on the role of the recipient, and write a return letter from that person. It forces clients out of their own emotional box and may bring some clarity to certain situations.

Another writing exercise is the composition of a narrative of the traumatic event/experience, its impact and the feelings it has generated. A person could donate large amounts of time or shorter amounts to this project. This narrative could be written in a personal fashion in the first person voice, or if distance is required due to the traumatic nature of the event, the client could write it as though it had happened to someone else. This form of writing belongs to a group of desensitization techniques which have proven helpful in PTSD.

## Poetry

Some believe that poetry may provide a more in-depth form of facilitation. Certain types of poetry use rhyme and rhythm and freely employ metaphors and similes. There is balance, symmetry, and sequence in the cadence of the words. This style of writing may generate a feeling of balance and orderliness at a time when the trauma has stolen a sense of control from the person's life. After the death of my 18-year-old son, Cliff, I expressed many of my memories and pain through the vehicle of poetry.

### Wilted Roses and Pious Platitudes

*Wilted roses and pious platitudes,*
*    How they harm, and blame, and destroy.*
*I listened each day as they came and they went;*
*    And I watched the effects on my boy.*

*The intent of the folks who offered the words,*
*    Was certainly good, right, and true.*
*But I noticed that Cliff was no better off;*
*    In fact, he seemed wearied and blue.*

*The comforters, armed with their empty clichés,*
*    Took aim and went straight for his heart.*
*They claimed that the Father had given them words,*
*    Their duty it was to impart.*

*When they needed to talk, and expound, and advise,*
*    Cliff listened to all that they said.*
*Then thanked them for coming, and offering God's words,*

*After all . . . they claimed to be led.*

*They rarely listened to my son,*
   *Though the thoughts he expressed were quite rare,*
*But they didn't mind using his limited strength;*
   *And I questioned: "Do they really care?"*

*When they asked how he felt and he honestly spoke,*
   *They suddenly seemed to go deaf.*
*The subject would change or the interest would shift;*
   *And frequently, the comforter left.*

*Then quietly, after the clamor was gone,*
   *We'd reflect on the message they aired.*
*And this thought just kept coming and coming again;*
   *It was really my son who had cared.*

*"Mom, I know they mean well, but they don't meet my need*
   *And from them I've got to be free.*
*My strength is near gone, still I hear what they say;*
   *But why . . . don't they listen to me?"*

*Wilted roses and pious platitudes,*
   *How they harm, and blame, and destroy.*
*To this day I can see and feel their effects;*
   *But they no longer bother my boy!*

Dedicated to my son
William Clifford Taylor
Died—Nov. 3, 1978

## Eye Movement Desensitization Reprocessing (EMDR)

Eye movement desensitization reprocessing (EMDR) was developed by Francine Shapiro (1989) from a personal experience while taking a walk. She noticed that disturbing thoughts were calmed when her eyes shifted from left to right and right to left. From this initial observation, she began to use it in her clinical practice with much success. Shapiro (1989/1995) states that EMDR should be classified as accelerated information processing that utilizes bi-lateral stimulation of the brain.

EMDR has more scientific research as a trauma treatment than any other method, except for medications. Because of its proven track record and its rapid response rate, it has become a popular technique. It began with eye movements. However; other methods such as a moving light bar, saccadic ear tones, hand pulsers and tapping are also effective. The theory behind the process is still unclear, but the results testify to the effectiveness of the treatment.

van der Kolk, Burbridge, and Suzuki (1997) conducted an important study using neuroimaging to pinpoint affected brain areas while EMDR is being performed. Their study agrees with Bremner's (2000) study and others regarding decreased hippocampus volume in PTSD clients.

This decreased volume is related to the increased activation of the amygdala, the emotional part of the brain. The hippocampus portion is a "cognitive map" and assists in information processing. van der Kolk showed that PTSD symptoms were mediated by increased activation of the anterior cingulate and the prefrontal area, which distinguishes between real threats and past trauma cues that are no longer relevant.

Shapiro (1998) poses the following explanation for her treatment's success:

> . . . negative life experiences of trauma are those which upset the biochemical balance of the brain's physical information processing system. This imbalance prevents the information processing from proceeding to a state of adaptive resolution with the result that the perceptions, emotions, beliefs, and meanings derived from the experiences are, in effect, 'locked' in the nervous system. The EMDR methodology, as a form of Accelerated Information Processing, may unblock the brain's information processing system through a number of ways.

Bessel van der Kolk performed a large National Institutes of Health study on the effectiveness of EMDR. It found that with a one-time adult onset trauma EMDR was the best treatment of any that had been published. Even today, it is still considered an extremely effective treatment.

Because of the importance of a client's interpretation in regard to healing, EMDR becomes an important technique. The following steps explain the process.

1. A client identifies a traumatic memory and a visual image or picture that accompanies it.

2. A Subjective Units of Distress (SUDs) rating is given by the client on a scale between 0–10, with 0 meaning no disturbance when thinking of or picturing the trauma and 10 being the most disturbance imaginable.

3. A safe place or person is established so that the client can temporarily rest in that pleasant memory if the trauma becomes overwhelming.

4. A negative cognition (belief) that is attached to the picture is defined. Example: "I'm defenseless, I allow people to take advantage of me, I'm worthless, etc."

5. A positive cognition is explored as to what the client would like to believe regarding the self or the situation. Example: "I'm able to defend myself." "I'm assertive and I stand up for myself." "I am a worthwhile, valuable person."

6. The client decides how true the positive cognition feels at the moment. It is rated on a scale of 0–7, with 7 being a totally believable statement and 0 being non-believable.

7. A body scan is occasionally conducted throughout the process to determine what the client may be experiencing. If it is too stressful, the client will use the safe place for calming down. The therapy can always be stopped at any time. The client is given the control.

8. The client begins the process by tracking the therapist's fingers as they move from left to right and right to left between 18 to 24 inches. Each left/right-right/left movement constitutes a set. Approximately 24 sets of eye movements are performed. (Other methods can be used such as a light bar, ear phones, tactile stimulation, and tapping on the client's left and right hands, shoulders, or knees in a rhythmic manner.) At the beginning of the tracking, the client is asked to visualize the traumatic image and repeat the negative cognition. Then the process takes over,

and the brain does its own healing. There is no talking during the eye movement time.

9. The therapist stops after the desensitizing eye movements and checks in with the client. "What's happening?" Client gives brief statement, and therapist says, "Stay with that or go with that memory." Then eye movements begin again.

10. After several sets of eye movement, the therapist checks by having the client view the original trauma picture and rate it from 0 to 10 on the SUDs rating. It may de-escalate as the disturbance decreases. The therapist continues the eye movements until the distress level is at least 1 or 0.

11. The positive cognition is than installed by the client repeating the desired belief to the self and sets of eye movements are continued until the new cognition is at a 6 or 7 believability level.

## CLIENT-DIRECTED EYE MOVEMENT TECHNIQUE

With minor issues or perhaps with hyperarousal control, clients can use the eye movement technique for themselves. They should never attempt to process a major trauma concern alone. That requires the facilitation of a therapist.

The concept of subjective units of distress (SUDs) must first be understood by the client before proceeding to the technique itself. The SUDs level is a subjective measurement from 0–10 that determines the amount of distress the client is experiencing. The ratings are usually viewed by EMDR specialists as a range of numbers between 0–10 which describes the disturbance of the emotion. The lower numbers 0–1 indicate no distress or minimal distress and the number 10 reveals the highest imaginable distress.

Clients can interpret for themselves the severity of the emotions that fall in between the highest and lowest range. After clients evaluate their level of disturbance, they then visualize a disturbing picture/image or identify a bodily sensation or emotion that represents the distress. While viewing this picture and feeling the bodily or emotional disturbance, they move the eyes rapidly from left to right and right to left. This movement constitutes a set and should take about one second. The client can use from 24 to 30 sets, at a range of approximately one and one half to two feet apart for the left to right/right to left movement. Clients could use their knees as a viewing mark if nothing in the room will work. After the eye movements, the client can determine by measuring the SUDs level if some of the distress, anxiety, or emotional pain has decreased. If not, they continue the eye movements until they have achieved as much improvement as possible.

The therapist may use the standard EMDR process of instructing the client to follow the fingers of the therapist in the back and forth procedure as a teaching tool. If the client experiences a decrease in the problem, then they know it will work for them. Clients are then encouraged to use it on their own for symptom control. Empowerment of this nature is greatly needed by some clients because their loss of control in life has severely disempowered them or placed them in a victim position.

## EMOTIONAL FREEDOM TECHNIQUES (EFT)

Emotional freedom techniques (EFT), designed by Gary Craig (1995), is a therapy with its roots in ancient Chinese medicine and the modern science of applied kinesiology. This therapy uses acupuncture points and the theory that all disease, physical or emotional, comes from blockage in the energy system. Tapping or massaging these points frees up the blockage. EFT teaches a simple recipe which can be applied to a wide variety of problems. Simple phobias are corrected in minutes, depressions lift, anxieties are calmed, and pain is reduced or disappears altogether.

Each year we learn more about how our brain functions. We now know that flashbacks from trauma are a result of over-activity in the right brain (amygdala) and under-activity in the left brain (Broca's area) leading to an inability to make cognitive/behavioral changes in the emotional response to an event from long ago.

Dr. Candace Pert, a research scientist who discovered the receptor sites for opiates in 1972, continued her research in the area of peptides (1997). Her research shows that peptides have the same capacity for communication, as do the neurotransmitters in the brain. However, peptides reside not only in the brain, but throughout the body and in every organ. She mapped clusters of peptides in the areas of the body that have been used as acupuncture points for thousands of years. She theorized that the energy meridians described by the Chinese are actually the pathways used by the peptides to run the immune system in the body. Her research shows the body gives messages to the brain and the brain gives messages to the body with equal authority. She described this as *"mindbody"* or *"bodymind."* Her explanation puts science behind applied kinesiology (muscle testing) and acupuncture, the two theories used in EFT.

EFT is simple, can be taught to someone in a single session, and does no harm. It does not require specific training in psychology to be used successfully. There are five points on the face, two on the body, and five on the hand. Gary Craig (1995) developed EFT after completing all available training in thought field therapy (TFT). He simplified TFT and formatted his "Basic Recipe" so that it can be learned quickly and remembered easily. In addition, this is a tool that can be used in any setting. (Brickner, 1999)

---

**Tapping Sites and Sequence**

| | | |
|---|---|---|
| EB | = | Beginning of the Eyebrow |
| SE | = | Side of the Eye |
| UE | = | Under the Eye |
| UN | = | Under the Nose |
| Ch | = | Chin (crevice) between lip and chin |
| CB | = | Beginning of the Collar Bone (1 inch down) |
| UA | = | Under the Arm (about 6 inches down) |
| Th | = | Thumb (outside area next to nail) |
| IF | = | Index Finger (outside area next to nail) |
| MF | = | Middle Finger (by nail facing index finger) |
| BF | = | Baby Finger (by nail facing ring finger) |
| KC | = | Karate Chop (side of hand below baby finger) |

---

Tap each point five-seven times working your way down the face to the collar bone, under the arm, then thumb and fingers. Either left or right side of body can be used for tapping. Focus on the disturbing event, thought, or feeling while tapping the 12 designated points.

This treatment also uses the technique of *psychological reversal.* Failure of the emotional freedom technique treatment can be caused by negative self-incriminating thinking. To reverse a negative effect a person must use a neutralizing affirmation such as: *"Even though I can't control my physiological arousal, I deeply and completely accept myself."* The person would repeat the affirmation three times while rubbing the sore spot. The sore spot is also referred to as the "pledge spot" since it's located where one would place their hand for the Pledge of Allegiance. There are two "sore spots" in your upper left and upper right regions of the chest. Find a U shaped notch at the top of your sternum (breastbone). From the top of that notch go down 3 inches toward your navel and over 3 inches to the left (or right). You should now be in the upper left (or right) portion of your chest. If you press vigorously in that area (within a 2 inch radius) you will feel a spot that feels tender, it is referred to as the sore spot. Another technique would be to tap the karate chop spot, which is the outside portion of the hand below the little finger. This technique clears the energy system and allows the tapping sequence to fulfill its task.

Emotional freedom techniques (EFT) can serve as a supplemental stabilization intervention, particularly in the area of physiological control. EFT is helpful in providing a sense of self control for trauma victims. Since trauma produces helplessness and a feeling of being out of control, any measure of control can be empowering. Because trauma victims may view their body as an out-of-control enemy, the physiological responses need to submit to the survivor's control. As mentioned earlier, survivors administer the tapping sequence to themselves, thus allowing self-regulation of becoming calmer and less disturbed. They can use the SUDs rating system to determine the degree of severity and improvement.

## EMDR AND EFT

Some clinicians have found that the combination of EMDR and EFT amplifies the benefits of therapy. EFT appears to supplement and enhance the rapid response rate of EMDR treatment. It also provides physiological control of disturbing body memories. Some proponents of EMDR believe that EMDR therapy can be useful in the reintegration of the fragmented self as well as in resolving the trauma. Since EMDR is accelerated information processing, it is logical to assume that if symptoms of the trauma have been reduced in a few sessions, then personality issues such as the fragmented self, should also show improvement. This improvement in personality problems may occur as a result of a change in the client's worldview. Trauma clients have a distorted view of the world and EMDR provides them with a more realistic one. EFT provides additional physiological stability while EMDR is solving trauma issues and perhaps integrating the shattered fragments of personality.

## RESOURCE DEVELOPMENT AND INSTALLATION

Andrew Leeds (1999) originated resource development and installation and believes that it contributes crucial elements to the treatment of PTSD and other trauma-based conditions. This self-enhancing and strengthening technique enables the client to acquire a more stable ego structure. This technique is frequently used in conjunction with the standard EMDR protocol. Leeds theorizes that positive resources (positive memories) are normally acquired in childhood through nurturing, supportive parents. Children develop healthy self objects relations or self esteem from meaningful relationships with primary care givers. Some clients may not have been privileged to develop these supportive internal systems and they need that inner strengthening before they can work on traumatic memories or they need these resources while processing difficult situations. Otherwise the client may be retraumatized.

A client is asked to identify a quality in the self that needs strengthening, a difficult life circumstance, a belief that needs changing, or a maladaptive schema. The client then thinks of a positive experience with good feelings and brings that affect into the difficult situation, which hopefully assists in minimizing, or offsetting the negative feeling. If a client can't find a positive memory or feeling, they can think of or visualize a powerful person effectively interacting in their negative memory.

Another option is the incorporation of a symbolic representation of the needed resource. For instance, an abused frightened little girl who was frequently locked in a dark closet might imagine that a loving nurturing person was in there with her, thus minimizing some of the fear and isolation. If a person isn't available as a resource, the little girl might choose a kind protective lion. When the abuser opened the door, perhaps to perpetrate additional abuse, the child could visualize the lion standing in front of her and scaring the attacker away. Any strengthening resource, person, or animal can assist the client in offsetting some of the intolerable emotions that may accompany the processing of the traumatic memory.

An additional technique attaches a positive, affirming statement to a pleasant visual image. For instance, Rita felt unloved by her earthly father, but she could effectively use her faith in Jesus as a resource. She visualized herself sitting in a beautiful flower garden with Jesus gazing lovingly at her with gentle compassionate eyes. While visualizing this image she would affirm to herself,

*"I am precious"* or *"I am loved."* Eye movements would seal this image and affirmation together. While using EMDR to overcome the negative memory and affect, she would bring this positive reinforcement into the process as needed. Resource development and installation can be as creative as required, but is definitely a valuable supplement to EMDR.

## VISUAL IMAGERY

Visual images are either pleasant or unpleasant pictures in the mind that evoke various emotions associated with the scene that is being experienced. All images stimulate changes in the client's physiological state which are beneficial or detrimental. If a client is imagining herself resting by a babbling brook under the flowering branches of a pink dogwood tree, then that scene probably produces a calming effect on her physiological condition. If the image contains sights of a traumatic situation, then the bodily state is aroused and ready for action.

Clients can be taught to construct meaningful images that generate a relaxed state, even if it exists only for a short period of time. Trauma clients already know the power of images since their mind and memories are bombarded by intrusive content that they wish they didn't remember. Imagery can serve as a positive form of dissociation if the client can discover safe or relaxing places they can visit in their mental trips. Perhaps completely unfamiliar images would be helpful, so as not to stir up any reminders of the trauma. For instance, the client could project herself into a foreign country, or see herself on a mountain top (since she's not a hiker) or visualize herself in a refreshing botanical garden where there are few reminders of the familiar. Healthy dissociating in this manner can provide a short reprieve, or mini-vacation, from the constancy of the trauma.

## LOGOTHERAPY

Dr. Viktor Frankl (1959), a psychiatrist, originated logotherapy from his experiences as a prisoner in the Auschwitz concentration camp. He believes that a search for meaning is part of the essence of our human spirit and essential for survival. Trauma survivors seem to know intuitively that their prolonged and tedious pathway will take them on a search for meaning. Frankl explains that survivors of the Nazi concentration camps were stripped of everything except the last human freedom: *"The ability to choose one's attitude in a given set of circumstances."* In comparing those who survived and those who died in the concentration camps, Frankl discovered that the survivors had managed to find a meaning to life even in those humiliating and devastating circumstances. Their attitude made the difference in the life or death quest. Frankl (1984) also explains that each person must find his or her own personal meaning, and that meaning cannot be transferred from one person to another. At different points in life and at various ages, the meaning can vary. Any personal suffering sets humans on a quest for meaning.

Frankl uses the term *"tragic optimism,"* which he defines as the ability to transform suffering into a meaningful experience and to acquire a positive outlook on life's traumatic events. Not all clients will be able to achieve Frankl's honorable goals; however, considerable progress can be made if clients purpose in their hearts the creation of something notable from their pain. Numerous organizations were born from traumatic circumstances. Mothers Against Drunk Drivers (MADD) is one such organization. It was started by Candy Lightner whose young daughter was killed by a drunk driver. The Grief Recovery Institute is another. It was born out of the pain of personal losses from its two founders, John James and Russell Friedman. Heartbeat, a group of suicide survivors, was started by LaRita Archibald following the suicide of her 24-year- old son. Some trauma survivors may start a support group; others may write a book, poem, or music. The meaning and creativity that comes forth is as unique as the individual himself.

Dr. Frankl (1984) summed it up in the following statement: *"To weave these slender threads of a broken life into a firm pattern of meaning and responsibility is the object and challenge of logo therapy."* It has been said, and it certainly applies to trauma survivors, *"Search for meaning, not happiness, and happiness may follow as a byproduct."*

## VISUAL/KINESTHETIC DISSOCIATION (V/KD)

Although most dissociation is viewed as a detrimental side effect of trauma, visual/kinesthetic dissociation (V/KD) is a therapeutic form of dissociation. V/KD has its roots in neurolinguistic programming and employs a "distancing" effect both for visual and kinesthetic stimulants. It can be used effectively to process material that is so traumatic that the client might dissociate in an attempt to bear it. The distancing effect enables the client to process the visual and kinesthetic aspects of the trauma from a less provocative viewpoint.

The following basic steps can easily be applied.

1. The therapist instructs the client to pretend she is sitting in a movie theatre which features her life on the screen. Perhaps the client may choose to view the film in black and white to make it less real or threatening. The therapist will be upstairs in the projection room running the film.

2. The client will view some scenes that existed immediately before the trauma and led up to it.

3. When the film reaches the time and place of the trauma, the client will quickly vacate her seat and float up into the projection room with the therapist. The change in location provides *distance* and *support* for the client, thus dissociating the client from the event.

4. The client is asked to view the person who is down there on the screen (who, of course, is self-experiencing the trauma). The client is now observing as though the trauma was happening to someone else. If it was a childhood trauma, the therapist might say, *"see that little girl at the appropriate age. For instance, visualize 3-year-old Alice riding her tricycle. She sees the dog, tries to run in the house, but gets bitten on her leg. See the frightened face of little Alice as the dog bites her."* The therapist leads the client all the way through the trauma.

5. The therapist may now request the client to rewind the movie as quickly as possible, within a few seconds. In other words, the client views the movie backwards. Alice screams and looks frightened, she is bitten by the dog, the dog is running backwards, Alice is running away from the house, etc.

6. The therapist asks the client if she has rewound it to the best of her ability. The rapidity of the procedure often enables the client to remove herself from the picture and obtain her freedom. Sometimes a piece of humor or bizarreness may even surface. If clients can dissociate from their feelings, they may not receive the emotional trigger from the amygdala, which is the usual PTSD response. The rapidity of this process may change or bypass the resultant feeling, which frees them from reliving the experience.

7. The therapist now asks if the client can sit in a seat close to the front of the theatre and view the movie. The client tries it and the therapist asks, *"Are there areas you didn't notice before?"* Discussion ensues. Sometimes a client may want to fast forward and run through it; or maybe they want to process one scene at a time. At any rate, the fast movement of this

technique hopefully bypasses the feelings of the amygdala and frees the person from the accompanying PTSD emotional response.

## TRAUMATIC INCIDENT REDUCTION (TIR)

French and Harris (1998) state that traumatic incident reduction:

> . . . is a procedure intended to render benign the consequences of past traumatic events. Used correctly and in suitable circumstances, it eliminates virtually all of the symptoms of PTSD and is capable of resolving a host of painful and unwanted feelings and emotions that have not surrendered to other interventions.

TIR requires flexible therapeutic sessions in that the therapist or facilitator desires to have the client reach an end point, which results in better feelings. It is not unusual for a session to continue for 2 to 3 hours. The ideal situation would bring the client to a resolution with accompanying relief, brightening of facial features, and positive feelings in one session. The average session is about an hour and a half.

The basic steps are explained by French and Harris (1998) in their book, *Traumatic Incident Reduction* (TIR). The following basic TIR is the form used most frequently with traumatized clients. It consists of the following steps:

## BASIC TIR

1. *Consulting your client's interests, you select an incident to "run" or address.* Of course, in almost any case presenting with—and because of—a known, single-incident trauma such as a rape or a plane crash, this assessment is essentially done before you have begun, and the presenting incident is the one you will be running with your client.

2. *Find out where the incident happened.* You may get responses such as, "It was when we lived in Virginia," "It happened at Mom's house," "I was on the red eye flight from California," or "We were at Uncle Jack's farm." Any response indicating a place is acceptable.

3. *Find out how long the incident lasted.* Responses such as, "It lasted for 15 minutes," "I was in it for over an hour," "We were only there for a

few moments," or "It was just long enough for me to smoke a cigarette," would all be acceptable.

4. *Have your client focus on the moment the incident occurred.* You are asking your client to prepare for the TIR viewing by putting attention on the beginning of the incident.

5. *Have your client close his/her eyes (if it is comfortable to do so).* Closing eyes often helps the viewer "see" the incident more clearly by removing the distractions of the environment.

6. *Ask your client to describe the scene at the moment when the incident began.* This begins the description of the incident but it is only the beginning moment (to set the stage, so to speak).

7. *Have your client silently (re) "view" the incident from beginning to end.* Before your client begins to tell what happened, (s)he must put it into perspective. This silent viewing helps.

8. *Have the client tell you what happened.* Your client's answer to this instruction may be a spare outline, or it may be very detailed.

9. *Repeat steps 4, 7, and 8.*

From this point, you facilitate the viewing by having the client repeat the cycle of going to the start of the incident, moving through it silently to the end, and then telling you what happened (steps 4, 7, and 8) until the client reaches an end point.

Although the process seems simple, TIR does require special training and the Institute in Florida can be contacted as to dates and places of training. *CBC Press LLC, 2000 Corporate Blvd. N.E., Boca Raton, FL 33431. Reprinted with permission from CRC Press LLC 1999, Traumatic Incident Reduction (TIR), Gerald D. French & Chrys J. Harris, Boca Raton, FL.

## EXPOSURE THERAPY

Exposure therapy is a form of desensitization where the client is systematically exposed to a feared memory, object, or anxiety-provoking situation. One painful situation in life such as little Alice being bitten by a dog, may set up a conditioned anxiety response whenever she is exposed to a similar painful stimulus. Since Alice experienced a traumatizing canine attack with several bite marks from a friend's dog in the past, then even as an adult she may approach all dogs in the present as fearsome objects. If Alice had been attacked several times by the friend's dog, then the memory would be heightened and strengthened. Of course, the anxiety levels would greatly increase with each repeated assault. Alice would have acquired some automatic thoughts in the presence of this animal. *"See dog, get bit"* might become the dominating thought pattern. Even if she saw two harmless tiny puppies bouncing, tumbling, and rolling around with each other, the fear/anxiety response could surface. It is possible that this conditioned response would generalize itself to other animals as well, such as cats and kittens.

Even if the attacking dog was placed in a cage with secure locks, Alice would express discomfort in that dog's presence. Her intellect would tell her she is safe but the automatic thought would generate the conditioned response of fear and anxiety. Alice may live by the dictates of *"see dog, get bit."* She won't visit friends with dogs, jog in the nearby park where people walk their dogs, or garden in her front yard where neighbors' dogs would approach her.

Desensitization in the form of exposure therapy could assist Alice. The natural tendency would be to avoid all dogs, the therapeutic advice would be the opposite. She should gradually begin to approach dogs in a careful calculated manner. The therapist could begin by exposing her to pictures of dogs, perhaps fluffy innocent looking puppies. The next step might be viewing a short clip of a video with a child playing with a puppy. Perhaps brief exposure to a caged and tiny, friendly puppy with a wagging tail and wiggly body would then follow. Petting the back end of the puppy while the mouth is muzzled could increase the exposure at another session. Gradually Alice would increase the exposure by petting the puppy without a muzzle, and when comfortable could begin exposure work with larger dogs.

Imaginal exposure is another facet of this therapy. Revisiting a traumatic memory in a safe environment reduces the negative impact of the event. Harry, a Vietnam veteran, discovered that he had difficulty picnicking at a state park with his wife and children. Picnicking was a family outing that he had previously enjoyed and was surprised at his traumatic response to this seemingly innocuous outing. The family spread a blanket on the ground by a babbling brook just a short distance off the road. A rambunctious teenage boy raced by and his car backfired. This auditory stimulation set up a chain of events that were unexpected by Harry. The creek became a ditch where soldiers hid and exchanged gun fire with the enemy. The picnic blanket transformed itself into a covering for dead comrades. Harry relived the horror of the war experience and was visibly shaken. He sought counseling and repeatedly revisited the Vietnam experience with all the sights and sounds in a safe environment with the counselor. The imagined exposure gradually desensitized him.

## GESTALT

Gestalt therapy, originated by Fritz Perls (1969), is a treatment which broadens a person's awareness of himself. It uses memories, emotions, bodily sensations, experiences of the past, etc. In short, everything that could contribute to the person's forming a meaningful configuration of awareness is an acceptable part of the therapy process.

The *"empty chair"* or the *"invisible person in the chair"* technique has been highly popularized as a means of facilitating unexpressed or repressed emotion. For instance, Jerry could pretend that the chosen person (living or deceased) is seated in front of him and he would initiate a conversation, thus facilitating the needed expression. It can be a one-way conversation or Jerry can role play the other person in addition to himself.

In relationship to trauma or PTSD, a client may choose to put the *"numbness"* in an empty chair and give it a voice. The client may query the lack of feeling and ask what purpose it serves. The client may play the part of numbness and speak for it, thus providing awareness for the self. The startle response, hyperalertness, nightmares, or any symptoms could be challenged and explored with the empty chair technique.

It is also important to recognize that the self consists of roles we play. Roles demystify labels such as dissociative identity disorder (DID). It normalizes the split parts of the self. Fragmented parts of the self could be placed in the chair and their purpose and character investigated. From this awareness work, the client may view various personalities as expressions of the core self and not as separate entities. These parts can then be integrated into the core self.

Frequently, abused children or women lack assertiveness skills, and their survival was based on submission. That requirement squelched the self-protective mechanisms and emotions that normally would have surfaced. Role playing can strengthen their ability to stand up for themselves and to vent the anger and other accompanying emotions.

## STEPHEN PORGES' POLYVAGAL SYSTEM THERAPIES

Dr. Porges, (2011), states that, "Music has been used to calm, to enable feelings of safety, to build a sense of community, and to reduce the social distance between people." Music therapy provides a novel approach that can help physical and mental health. Listening to music, singing, and playing a musical instrument involve interactions between a therapist, client and music. This therapy improves social engagement behaviors and facilitates the regulation of bodily and behavioral states in a traumatized client. Our nervous system is continually evaluating risk in the environment. Porges states: *"The way we react to specific acoustic frequency bands that constitute music is determined by the same neural circuits that we use to evaluate risk in our environment."* Therefore, we can use music to generate various emotional states. This also places importance on how voice tones of human beings affect one another.

Bessel van der Kolk, M.D. (2013) emphasizes other forms of therapies that would complement the polyvagal theory. For example, yoga programs have worked well for chronically traumatized women because they learn to calm themselves by managing their breathing and challenging their dissociated bodies to move into difficult physical poses. This allows them to get in touch with their bodies. Another technique would be theatre where traumatized people act out various parts and perform definitive movements. Chi qong-based therapies have also worked well for survivors of tsunamis, earthquakes, and political violence. Breath exercises, body movements (chi qong, tai chi, tae kwon do, and yoga) as well as rhythmic activities such as kendo drumming and davening may be looked upon with favor. Dr. van der Kolk explains that these methods cause beneficial shifts in autonomic states. Therapists may want to use play, rough and tumble behaviors to develop adaptive defensive and aggressive behaviors as a method of moving people out of their fight or flight state into a loving and mutually engaged mobilization.

It's also noteworthy that some therapists are developing techniques for moving individuals out of their freezing state by having them hold ice in their hands or dip their face in ice water. This shocks them out of the numb, frozen state into a consciousness of reality. As time emerges, other techniques will result from trial experimentation.

## TREATMENTS AND TECHNIQUES FOR DISSOCIATION

First the client must realize that he or she is using some form of dissociation. Awareness and education are needed here. Generally there is a trauma trigger such as a person, a place, an event, that causes a physiological, mental or emotional reaction. Becoming aware of these triggers can help the person prepare for them. Self-regulation techniques can assist, such as meditation or mindfulness. Relaxation, breathing techniques, stress reduction techniques and supportive loving people are also helpful. Staying grounded or staying in the present may have to be practiced. Each client can create methods that work for him or her.

Kate, when feeling she was going to dissociate, would open her cell phone and look at a picture of her grand-daughter. Her attention then remained in the present on the granddaughter. Nick imagined the titles of his favorite books on the cocktail table at home and it kept him grounded. Each person can create their own method of focusing their attention on something else when tempted to dissociate. Allow me to bring dissociation into a clinical setting. It is likely that encountering traumatic material could cause many to dissociate during the counseling session. For instance, the clinician may have a beautiful bouquet of flowers on her desk. If the client dissociates, the clinician can repeatedly call the client's name. Because the client's name is so familiar to her, it may penetrate the fog. Then the client would be asked to describe the mixed bouquet of flowers. For example, she would describe the bright red rose; notice its beauty, and the way the petals unfurl around it. The clinician would then ask her to describe other flowers such as the yellow sweet pea with its blossoms that resemble lips. Any interesting object can serve as a stabilizing force: statues, pieces of art, pictures, sculptures. Sometimes a person can initiate a conversation with a loved one or friend which helps them not to space out. They can even talk out loud to themselves and describe their present surroundings. *A key word for a person on the verge of dissociating is NOTICE. If they are noticing, they will dissociate less.*

Bessel van der Kolk, in a 2013 interview, states that clients need stabilization, and *"feeling safe"* is the essential first step before processing the trauma. Some of the older treatments have resurfaced in popularity to assist with dissociation. EMDR, yoga, chi gong, touch, improvisational techniques are a sample of methods that help with dissociation. As mentioned earlier, Stephen Porges' polyvagal theory (2011) has led to techniques to alleviate dissociation such as holding ice in your hands or dipping your face in ice water. A creative therapist can give homework assignments to the client to *"retrain the mind."* For example, Steve is planning to mow his grass. He could be instructed to notice the length of the blades of grass in the strip he will be mowing. After cutting, he would notice the shorter length of the blades of grass. As he continues to mow, he will notice, notice, notice! Remember that noticing is the opposite of dissociating! Let's look at another simple example. Marjorie is making a salad for dinner. She can use the ingredients to build her focus and concentration skills. She will notice the redness and shape of the tomato as she cuts it, as well as the orange and roundness of the carrot. Noticing whatever a person is doing keeps the mind in the present and away from dissociating.

## New Therapeutic Trends and Techniques

In a PESI interview with Bessel van der Kolk (2012) he discusses new frontiers of trauma treatment. He explains that, *"The memory imprints of trauma are held in physical sensations, bodily states and habitual action patterns. This causes the entire human organism to continuously react to current experiences as a replay of the past."* Recovery means bringing the traumatic experience to an end in every aspect of the human organism. Some of the treatments and techniques espoused by van der Kolk and other trauma experts take us back to the ancient arts and other techniques as opposed to our conventional earlier talk therapies. He suggests yoga, mindfulness, rhythms such as Stephen Porges' music therapy, Francine Shapiro's EMDR, neurofeedback, Pat Ogden's sensorimotor psychotherapy, martial arts, internal family systems therapy and theater are helpful when used with the appropriate client. These therapies and techniques assist the person to live in the present, rather than dissociating or staying in the past.

Van der Kolk completed a study on the effectiveness of yoga with traumatized people. It showed how difficult it was for traumatized people to get back into their bodies and feel relaxed and safe, even though some parts of the practice (*Shavasana*—the blissful part) are difficult because it is one important technique that helps them to sense their body. With these non-verbal methods we can bypass the verbal language and access the sensate dimension. Any activity or technique such as martial arts, qi gong, craniosacral work, Feldenkrais technique, dancing, moving, singing, Rolfing, or exercise that engages the body in a mindful way will heal some traumatized brain areas. Many people are in a traumatic relationship with their bodies, and they need to feel safe in their bodies. Movement serves also as an antidote to helplessness. Peter Levine (1997) has shown that stress hormones need to be discharged. If they're not discharged, they keep the person in an unhealthy hyper aroused state. People need to move in order to heal and discharge the stress hormones. Traumatized people have many cellular memories and they can only be released through movement. Van der Kolk (2013), shared about being involved with a Shakespeare program for juvenile delinquents where the judge gives kids a choice between going to prison or becoming a Shakespearean actor. The young people who choose the acting come to life and feel valued as an actor and a person who is able to talk. They are applauded and validated and can take on a different persona. Imagine a young man or woman who had been victimized playing a role as a hero or heroine, talking and acting like one. It can begin to exchange their helpless feelings for powerful ones. Theater can be a change agent for many people.

For those of us who are therapists or professional caregivers, we need to think outside of the box. Healing occurs in many different ways. To be the best we can be, we need to use a variety of tools. We have the privilege of touching many precious lives in numerous creative ways. Let's try something new or perhaps something old that has come full circle.

## OUR UNCONSCIOUS COMMUNICATIONS

Numerous theorists such as Schore (2007), Fisher (2011), Porges (2011), and Scaer (2005) emphasize our unconscious attachment/connection and effect with our clients. It then behooves us to communicate with facial expressions, eyes, body, feelings, tone of voice as well as verbally. Scaer (2005) describes implicit communications embedded within the therapist-client relationship. Many features of social interaction are nonverbal, consisting of subtle variations of facial expression that set the tone for the content of the interaction. Body postures and movement patterns of the therapist also may reflect emotions such as disapproval, support, humor, and fear. Tone and volume of voice, patterns and speed of verbal communication, and eye contact also contain elements of subliminal communication and contribute to the unconscious establishment of a safe, healing environment. Fisher (2010) explains that these are right brain communications and they convey the personality of the therapist more than conscious verbalizations. Schore (2003) describes the nature of implicit and explicit processes:

> During the treatment, the empathic therapist is consciously, explicitly attending to the patient's verbalizations in order to objectively diagnose and rationalize the patient's dysregulating symptomatology. The therapist is also listening and interacting at another level, an experience—near subjective level, one that implicitly processes moment-to-moment socioemotional information at levels beneath awareness.

How does a therapist work with what is being communicated but not symbolized by words? Bucci (2002) observes, "We recognize changes in emotional states of others based on perception of subtle shifts in their facial expression or posture, and recognize changes in our own states based on somatic or kinesthetic experience." These implicit communications are expressed within the therapeutic alliance between the client and therapist's right brain systems.

Mandal and Ambady (2004) state that:

> Human beings rely extensively on nonverbal channels of communication in their day-to-day emotional as well as interpersonal exchanges. The verbal channel, language, is a relatively poor medium for expressing the quality, intensity and nuancing of emotion and affect in different social situations . . . the face is thought to have primacy in signaling affective information.

Schore (2003) has explained that the left brain communicates its states to other left brains through conscious linguistic behaviors and the right nonverbally communicates its unconscious states to other right brains that are tuned to receive these communications. There seems to be a consensus that the concepts of transference and counter-transference represent a common ground for therapists with different theoretical orientations. Shuren and Grafman (2002) explain the right hemisphere:

> The right hemisphere holds representations of the emotional states associated with events experienced by the individual. When that individual encounters a familiar scenario, representations of past emotional experiences are retrieved by the right hemisphere and are incorporated into the reasoning process.

Fisher (2008) explains that facial indicators of transference are seen in visual and auditory affective cues quickly appraised from therapists' face. Jacobs (1994) tells us that counter-transference is similarly currently defined in nonverbal implicit terms as the therapists' *"autonomic responses are reactions on an unconscious level to nonverbal messages."* In summary, transference/counter-transference transactions thus represent nonverbal right brain mind body communications.

Fisher (2011) summarizes the impact of therapist and client communicating unconsciously from right brain to right brain. Obviously right brain work involves a deep commitment by the therapist and the client but will produce far better outcomes than applying rigid techniques or principles as in the past. We now can resemble the proper mother-infant attachment system and form a secure safe base attachment with our clients.

Tutte (2004) states that:

> Over the ensuing stages of the treatment, the sensitive empathic clinician's monitoring of unconscious process rather than content calls for right brain attention to her matching the patient's implicit affective-arousal states. The empathic therapist also resonates with the client's simultaneous implicit expressions of engagement and disengagement within the co-constructed intersubjective field. This in turn allows the clinician to act as an interactive regulator of the patient's psychobiological states.

## ATTACHMENT AND RELATIONSHIP STRATEGIES FOR THERAPISTS AND CAREGIVERS

1. Trust must build and testing must occur. Don't expect automatic trust, don't ask or expect to be trusted. Don't take mistrust personally. Use mistrust as a schema understanding. If client seems to trust too early, they may be placating you as a dangerous potential betrayer.

2. Do not blame the client for certain behaviors. The behaviors developed in some cases as protective strategies when the child learned or adapted to parents.

3. Be careful not to create shame in regard to trouble with failing symptoms and behavioral symptoms.

4. The therapist must be willing to maintain close connection and consistency.

5. The therapist should be more transparent. Get in it with them. Let your feelings show. Clients don't want to talk to a robot.

6. Consider using eye movement desensitization and reprocessing (EMDR). Trauma work is not just addressing the trauma, but addressing the beliefs and distorted perceptions around it. EMDR does both.

7. The therapist must have a contract and a plan to prevent suicide and self-destructive behavior, including people to call in emergency situations, etc.

8. The client must have a safe environment with people and the therapist.

9.  Teach clients to self-soothe with techniques such as diaphragmatic breathing. Avoiding chronic arousal is a big problem. Consistent trauma renders the person unable to modulate arousal; therefore they drink, use drugs, etc. Insomnia is frequent. Other problems occur such as: dissociation, flashbacks, spacing-out, depersonalization, inability to stay present and amnesic episodes. Reducing arousal, mindfulness and staying present must be in place before successful therapy can be employed.

10. Let the client figure out and make meaning for themselves whenever possible. Logo therapy may be useful. In essence it teaches the person to, *"make creative use out of the suffering."*

11. Tape record the session—client and therapist can listen together. Playback time may be useful for processing.

12. The therapist must establish a genuinely caring, freely chosen, fair to both parties, mutually attuned and mutually rewarding relationship. Some victims cannot imagine a relationship like that. The victim may assume that the therapist is setting them up for betrayal. Nevertheless, caring, connecting, and consistency will serve as a role model for a normal relationship.

13. Recognize areas of strength and resilience in traumatized individuals, as this will constitute the basis for a therapeutic alliance.

14. Group therapy can give supportive feedback to each other, and clients discover they have something of value to share, by being able to help another person.

15. Couple and family systems therapy help victims discover and build healthy relationships. They help develop new working models for trust and security within their most immediate relationships.

16. The therapist must not have an authoritative relationship. It should be trusting and collaborative. The victim may try to place the therapist in various untrustworthy roles.

17. Fostering clients' social engagement and regulatory abilities is a top priority.

18. The therapist's response to the client is essential. React quickly when client is expressing pain. The therapist needs to ask what to do to assist. If client is unsafe, do what is necessary to help them be safe. Example: if client needs air, open a window, turn on a fan if that is comfortable, go outside for fresh air, or practice deep breathing.

## Treatment for Developmental Trauma Disorder and Children with Complex PTSD

### Bessel van der Kolk, M.D.

1. It is imperative to provide safety and predictability in relationships.

2. Listen and help the child find words to express him/herself.

3. Children need vocabulary to express feelings. Give them words, choices, etc.

4. Give them pleasure and mastery. Since we only feel good about ourselves when we do something well, help them find competency. Examples: play the piano, engage in sports, sing, dance, crafts, sewing, art, drawing. Bring out their talent and help them obtain mastery in some area. Let them move in life and see it in a larger context. They must be able to feel that there is pleasure and fun in life, not just pain.

5. Structure time to help the child learn organizational skills.

6. Teach breathing techniques, Biodots, emotional freedom techniques (EFT), self-regulation, sports, music, etc. It makes the child feel more powerful.

7. Try neurofeedback or play a computer game. These both alter brain waves.

8. Use yoga, theater, body movement, and martial arts.

9. Teach meditation.

10. Safely allow the child to know what he knows, and be validated for it. He/she is visible and should be acknowledged.

11. Use Eye Movement Desensitization Reprocessing (EMDR). It has best outcome on a child. EMDR views trauma as a historical event.

12. Write music and songs about healing. Example: The child could be a rap specialist. They could use drumming, singing, etc.

13. Move the body—dance, run, breathe, play sports. Use movement that makes the child feel strong.

14. Traumatized children need safety, sameness and predictability in relationships. Don't shift them from person to person, from caregiver to caregiver. Be sure they have a few consistent loving caregivers.

15. Remember that we are wounded in relationships and can be healed in relationships. Ensure that meaningful relationships are built. Find relationships that provide constancy, love and consistency. Use people who will always be accessible when needed.

16. Help them learn to regulate themselves. Use yoga, martial arts, sports, music, dancing, etc. Any movement is healing.

17. Use body oriented therapies with them since memories are held on a cellular level.

18. Assist them in calming down. EMDR provides the best outcome of any therapies for processing trauma and self-regulation.

19. Introduce them to theatre. They can act out parts or write a play. Perhaps they can write a song, story or poem.

20. Notice what people already have, what resources, talents and skills they can use. Move, breathe, have fun, dance, laugh, play. Do anything safe that makes the child feel strong and powerful.

21. Tai chi calms the self and regulates the body. It also heals the body and the brain.

22. Safety first in every action. Avoid trauma related triggers. Avoid pursuits that remind them of trauma related triggers. Example: child afraid of bed, parents tied child in bed. Solution—make bed look like a boat or motorcar. Maybe put sleeper sofa in room. Example: child locked in closet. Use folding doors that won't lock.

23. They need to learn to react differently than their coping mechanisms have taught them. Example: isolate self or fight/flight/freeze reactions. Teach them new behaviors and ways to cope. Instead of fighting, work on better communication techniques and negotiations to solve their problem.

24. Give them as much control as possible. They react against rules and regulations and may see protective interventions as punishment. Example: wear your hat or coat, eat your vegetables, be in bed by 9:00pm. Anything new may be viewed as punishment, and caregivers, teachers or clinicians as perpetrators.

25. Reward them for adhering to difficult rules that may be viewed as punishment. Be sure the reward is something they really want or would like.

**26.** Give them multiple choices. Example: You can have Johnny over to play or you may play your video games or you may ride your bicycle with Steve. This eliminates dictatorial control to some degree.

**27.** Provide physical experiences which give them a feeling of being in charge. They need to be able to accomplish the goals they set for themselves. Their hyperarousal and numbing are deeply set. Children with frozen reactions need to move and explore their surroundings. It helps to awaken their curiosity. They'll avoid any activity that may unexpectedly become a trauma trigger. For example, a child who was tied to a bed wouldn't go to a slumber party. Neutral "fun" talks and physical games can give them a sense of what it feels like to be relaxed. Movement works as a constructive release for hyper aroused energy and gets them unstuck from the freezing state.

## LIFE SCRIPTS

A life script is a plan we chose for our lives when we are a child and will continue to act out through our lifetime. It is a lifetime *"repetitive compulsion."*

Each child develops a jumble of messages derived from parents and other influences. Some messages are survival conclusions, some helpful, some harmful, some irrelevant, some practical and some important. All the messages carry different weight and are believed by the child to varying degrees. Our scripts then have a large collection of conclusions, some of which continue to be useful, others not and some extremely damaging. A typical script-making age is between 4 and 7, yet even infants and babies are making important conclusions through intuition. Example: Between 3 – 8 months an infant will decide if the mother is good or bad, and if human beings in general are good or bad. A baby may feel "I need this person, but she doesn't need me." We carry these feelings into adulthood.

Script theory is based on the belief that children make conscious life plans in early childhood or early adolescence which influence and make the rest of their lives predictable.

From words and actions by parents and other influential figures, children may adopt a variety of positions about their worth and value such as:

I'm smart

I'm stupid

I'm powerful

I'm inadequate

I'm nice

I'm nasty

I'm an angel

I'm a devil

I never do anything right

I can't do anything wrong

I'm as good as anybody else

I don't deserve to live

When thinking of other people, they may conclude:

People will give me anything I want

Nobody will give me anything

People are wonderful

People are horrible

Someone will help me

People are out to get me

Everybody likes me

Nobody likes me

People are nice

Everybody's mean

Parents may send destructive messages to their children such as:

You're so lazy. You'll never amount to anything.

You must have come from a bad seed.

I'm ashamed of you. You've ruined our family reputation.

We'd have been better off without you.

You've cost us an arm and a leg.

You can't do that. Let me do it for you.

Hey, get lost. Go play in the street.

Don't cry, be a big boy.

Little girls should be seen, but not heard.

Children accept the evaluations given them by others. However, the child can change that evaluation by rewriting the script.

Betty was told she was a stupid, worthless child and she would always fail at anything in life. She could rewrite her script by stating, *"I'm an intelligent, worthwhile person and I am successful in my career and with my family."* She could make 3x5 cards with her new script and post them around the house, reading them aloud every time she saw them. She could also use EMDR as a way to build the new script into her mind. She might act in a more confident manner, which further installs the new script. She might mentally repeat the new script to herself throughout the day. She could also record her voice and play it back to herself while mentally imaging herself as being an intelligent, worthwhile career person and mother. Any technique that reinforces the new script image can be useful.

## SELF-ANALYSIS/LIFE SCRIPTING EVALUATION

### Decisions You Made Early in Life Now Rule Your Every Waking and Sleeping Moment!

Those decisions can lead to depression, suicide, drug addiction, alcoholism, and great unhappiness. It may cause you to feel powerless over your life course or render you unable to have a loving relationship with another human being. These early childhood decisions are called your *"life script."*

A script results from a childhood decision, which was premature and forced. It was made under pressure long before decisions can properly be made. The earlier the decision, the more serious or tragic the script. When a youngster's expectations of protection to develop aren't met, a script occurs. To the child, it seems as if alien forces are applying pressure against his growth. Unless he yields to these pressures, life becomes extremely difficult.

Since scripts are consciously willed decisions, they can be revoked by other consciously willed decisions. We can recognize our life script, break free of it, and take control of our life.

### Childhood Scenes

**Pretend that you are an infant or child and answer these questions:**

**1. Picture Your Mom**

    **a.** Where is the first place you see her?

    **b.** What is she doing?

    **c.** What is she saying?

    **d.** What would you change about your Mom?

    **e.** What does your Mom want you to be when you grow up?

    **f.** What was your Mom's main word of advice to you?

    **g.** When you did something good, what was your Mom's response to you?

    **h.** When you did something bad, what was your Mom's response to you?

    **i.** What was your Mom's favorite nickname for you and what did it mean to you?

## 2. Picture Your Dad

**a.** Where is the first place you see him?

**b.** What is he doing?

**c.** What is he saying?

**d.** What would you change about your Dad?

**e.** What does your Dad want you to be when you grow up?

**f.** What was your Dad's main word of advice to you?

**g.** When you did something good, what was your Dad's response to you? (Please give example.)

**h.** When you did something bad, what was your Dad's response to you? (Please give example.)

**i.** What was your father's favorite nickname for you and what did it mean to you?

3. **What is the Earliest Childhood Memory That You Can Recall?**

4. **What was Your Favorite Fairy Tale, Nursery Rhyme or Bible Story? Who were You in the Story?**

5. **What Would You Change about Yourself at 5 Years of Age?**

6. **Were You Named After Someone? Did You Like That Individual? Have You Patterned Yourself or Your Life After That Person?**

7. **Who Made the Major Decisions in Your Home?**

8. **What was the Happiest Experience You Had With One or Both of Your Parents?**

9. **What was the Saddest or Most Disappointing Experience You Had With One or Both of Your Parents?**

10. **If You Could Be Anyone You Desired, Who Would You Be?**

11. **List 10 Things You Couldn't Do at Your House. (This Covers Childhood to Adulthood.)**

    1.

    2.

    3.

    4.

    5.

    6.

    7.

    8.

    9.

    10.

12. **List 10 Things You were Supposed to Do in Your House. (This Covers Childhood to Adulthood.)**

    1.

    2.

    3.

    4.

    5.

    6.

    7.

    8.

    9.

    10.

**13. What Messages Did You Receive as to What Behaviors were Good or Bad or Normal or Abnormal for a Woman or a Man?**

**1.** A good _____

_____

_____

**2.** A good _____

_____

_____

**3.** A good _____

_____

_____

**4.** A good _____

_____

_____

**5.** A good _____

_____

_____

14. **Rewrite the Script as You Want It to Be. Example: Some women were scripted to believe they must take care of everybody and everything before they could rest or take care of themselves. Therefore, a woman with that negative script should write a new healthy script as the example shows.**

    **1.** A good woman can rest and take care of herself.

    **2.** A good _____

    _____

    _____

    **3.** A good _____

    _____

    _____

    **4.** A good _____

    _____

    _____

    **5.** A good _____

    _____

    _____

## Complex Post Traumatic Stress Disorder Treatment

Doctor Judith Herman has said there are three phases of treatment for complex traumatic stress disorder (CPTSD).

Phase One: Stabilization

Phase Two: Processing and Grieving of Traumatic Memories

Phase Three: Reconnection and Reintegration with the World

### A POSSIBLE TEST

Van der Kolk has developed a computerized Traumatic Antecedent Questionnaire (TAQ) which gathers information about the patient's resources, their competencies and feelings of safety with different people during their life. It also assesses traumatizing events through all developmental events including neglect, separations from significant others, secrets and emotional abuse, physical abuse, sexual abuse, witnessing others' traumas and exposure to alcohol and drugs. If you use this test, you'll have a history of resources and of traumatizing life events. Thus, we begin treatment by:

1. Establishing A Diagnosis That Prioritizes the Problems and
2. Design A Treatment Plan.

Most experts agree on the following treatment strategy (van der Kolk, McFarlane & Hart, 1996):

### Phase Oriented Treatment of Complex PTSD*

1. Symptom management: medications, dialectical behavior therapy, mindfulness training, stress inoculation training.
2. Create narratives.
3. Realize repetitive patterns.
4. Make connections between internal states and actions:
   - *Aggression*
   - *Sex*
   - *Eating*

- *Gambling*
- *Cutting self*

5. Identify traumatic memory nodes, followed by:
   - *Exposure therapy*
   - *EMDR*
   - *Body oriented work*

6. Learn interpersonal connections—12 step programs, negotiation of sharing responsibility and intimacy.

According to Courtois and Ford (2013), these "complex trauma" effects have significant implications for treatment, and a single intervention strategy and short term treatments were rarely sufficient to address the myriad of trauma symptoms. In their book titled, *Treatment of Complex Trauma*, they indicated that some cognitive-behavioral therapies (CBT) have led us to advances in the trauma field. They have given us therapies such as ". . . prolonged exposure (Foa, 2011), cognitive processing therapy (Resick & Schnicke, 1993), dialectical behavior therapy (Linehan, 1993), eye movement desensitization and reprocessing (Shapiro, 1995), and, for children, trauma-focused cognitive-behavioral therapy (Cohen, Mannarino, & Deblinger, 2006)." Courtois and Ford (2009) believe there is clearly a need for many more treatments, and clinicians are reconsidering the importance of a positive therapeutic relationship. Some older therapies, such as psychodynamic, client-centered, and more recently, relational components have recaptured our attention. These interpersonal elements contain the most consistently supported findings in the therapy outcome literature.

Many of the treatments in the Current Trends and Therapies section apply as treatments for CPTSD such as van der Kolk's suggestions of theater, EMDR, polyvagal therapies, breathing, music, dancing, etc. Please see other sections that more fully explain these therapies. All of the techniques that bond unconsciously with the right brain of the client, such as eye and facial expressions, tonal qualities, and body postures, are particularly relevant and receiving much popularity.

---

*Reprinted with permission from van der Kolk, B.A., McFarlane, A.C. & van der Hart, O. (1996). The Assessment and Treatment of Complex PTSD, Chapter 7, Traumatic Stress, Arlington, VA. American Psychiatric Press, 2001.

# CHAPTER SIX

# COMPASSION FATIGUE

## THE EFFECTS OF COMPASSION FATIGUE

Compassion fatigue (CT), also known as secondary traumatic stress, affects a broad range of health care professionals as well as others who provide a myriad of listening and support services. This condition occurs when professionals, families, friends, or caregivers are continually exposed to extreme emotional circumstances either directly or indirectly, in an attempt to treat or support traumatized people.

Because the effects of compassion fatigue are cumulative, caregivers may be unaware of this syndrome's ability to rob them of their energy, vitality, and resiliency. The pervasiveness of this phenomenon places the helping professions at high risk of sacrificing their own physical, mental, emotional, and spiritual well-being on the *altars of compassion*.

## COMPASSION FATIGUE AND BURNOUT

The logical question regarding the diagnosis of CF is whether or not it is the same condition as burnout. Maslach (1982) who developed the Maslach Burnout Inventory (MBI) provides an explanation for what he labeled as burnout. He indicates that this physical, mental, and emotional exhaustion is caused by a depletion of the ability to cope with one's environment. This inability results from having to meet high level demands in daily life. Maslach's definition relates primarily to an environmental condition that encompasses numerous factors. The term compassion fatigue differs from burnout in that it concentrates on the transfer of emotions from the primary victim to a secondary one.

Figley (1995) provides a further comparison between burnout and compassion fatigue. Burnout:

173

> ... emerges gradually .... STS (secondary traumatic stress) can emerge suddenly with little warning ... in contrast to burnout, there is a sense of helplessness and confusion, and a sense of isolation from supporters; the symptoms are often disconnected from real causes.

This concept of compassion fatigue is relatively new, entering our awareness with Joinson's (1992) article, "Coping with Compassion Fatigue" published in *Nursing* magazine. The article focused on describing the characteristics and behaviors of nurses who handled emergencies and developed compassion fatigue as a result.

Joinson is credited with the introduction of the term compassion fatigue, and others have contributed closely related concepts such as vicarious traumatization (McCann & Pearlman 1990) and secondary survivor (Remer & Elliott 1988b). Charles Figley (1995) popularized the term compassion fatigue when he used it as the title of his ground-breaking book. He also described this same phenomenon as secondary traumatic stress in his earlier writings.

Figley (1995) defines compassion fatigue or secondary traumatic stress as:

> The natural behaviors and emotions that arise from knowing about a traumatizing event experienced by a significant other—the stress resulting from helping or wanting to help a traumatized person.

## EXAMPLES OF COMPASSION FATIGUE BURNOUT SYMPTOMS

**Cognitive:** Lowered concentration, decreased self-esteem, apathy, rigidity, disorientation, perfectionism, minimization, preoccupation with trauma, thoughts of self-harm or harm to others.

**Emotional:** Powerlessness, anxiety, guilt, anger/rage, survivor guilt, shutdown, numbness, fear, helplessness, sadness, depression, emotional roller coaster, depleted, overly sensitive.

---

Compassion Fatigue Burnout Symptoms are reprinted by permission from Treating Compassion Fatigue (© 2002). Routledge/Taylor & Francis Books, Inc.

**Behavioral:** Inpatient, irritable, withdrawn, moody, regression, sleep disturbance, nightmares, appetite changes, hypervigilance, elevated startle response, accident proneness, losing things.

**Spiritual:** Questioning the meaning of life, loss of purpose, lack of self-satisfaction, pervasive hopelessness, anger at God, questioning of prior religious beliefs, loss of faith in a higher power, greater skepticism about religion.

**Personal Relations:** Withdrawal, decreased interest in intimacy or sex, mistrust, isolation from others, overprotectiveness as a parent, projection of anger or blame, intolerance, loneliness, increased interpersonal conflicts.

**Somatic:** Shock, sweating, rapid heartbeat, breathing difficulties, aches and pains, dizziness, increased number and intensity of medical maladies, other somatic complaints, impaired immune system.

**Work Performance:** Low morale, low motivation, avoiding tasks, obsession about details, apathy, negativity, lack of appreciation, detachment, poor work commitments, staff conflicts, absenteeism, exhaustion, irritability, withdrawal from colleagues.

Any of these symptoms could be signaling the presence of compassion fatigue or burnout.

## AVOIDING COMPASSION FATIGUE

Figley believes that this syndrome could be classified as secondary traumatic stress (STS) or in severe cases as secondary traumatic stress disorder (STSD). STS or STSD results from an intense and caring involvement with a traumatized person. In his 1995 book titled, *Compassion Fatigue*, he describes it as: "A state of tension and preoccupation with individual or cumulative trauma of clients as manifested in one or more ways: reexperiencing the traumatic events, avoidance/numbing or reminders of the event, (or) persistent arousal."

This description with the three clusters of reexperiencing, avoidance, and arousal sounds familiar in that they are Criterion B, Criterion C, and Criterion D of the DSM-IV-TR for PTSD. Of course, the DSM-5 has added a fourth cluster of alterations in negative cognitions and moods which also fulfills the compassion fatigue diagnosis.

Figley (1995) postulates that any individuals, (lay, volunteers, professional, or family) who are emotionally connected to the primary victim are vulnerable to developing secondary traumatic stress disorder. In regard to health care professionals, it is highly likely that we can "catch" it from our clients. A good relationship between client and clinician depends on the clinician's ability to convey compassion, in the process rendering the clinician susceptible to secondary traumatic stress. Numerous theories have surfaced in an attempt to explain the mechanism by which this syndrome is transmitted, but there is no conclusive proof. Figley (1995) has hypothesized that indeed it is the empathy level of the clinician that causes the transmission and that assumption has certainly been validated in the lives of traumatized clinicians. An additional contributing factor lies in the background of many clinicians and caregivers. Approximately two-thirds of them are trauma survivors. That position renders them susceptible for retraumatization if preventive strategies are not employed.

Not only does a clinician personally suffer from the effects of compassion fatigue, but the professionalism of the clinician declines as well. For instance, Baranowsky (2002) and Danielli (1984) explain that clinicians find it difficult to listen to the traumatic experiences of the client and they redirect the conversation to material that is less anxiety provoking for the clinician. The term for redirecting the conversation away from distressing information is called the silencing response. When used, it is indicative of the clinician's inability to handle the overwhelming nature of the client's story. Obviously, clinical efficiency is compromised at that point.

Self-assessment is essential for all caregivers in the field of traumatology. Periodic checkups with another competent professional can also assist with some objectivity. The Compassion Satisfaction/Fatigue Self-Test for Helpers developed by B. Hudnall Stamm and Charles R. Figley (1996) can be administered and self graded from time to time. Copies can be made of the test which allows the clinician to track the experience and compare scores, however, sale of the test is prohibited. Please see the Appendix for a copy of the test.

All elements measured are significant and will provide information in three areas: compassion, job satisfaction, and fatigue. It is important to recognize and evaluate the impact of job satisfaction in addition to compassion and fatigue. Job satisfaction can serve as a powerful antidote against the effects of compassion fatigue.

It is important for clinicians to learn to recognize and combat the deleterious effects of STS, hopefully preventing the emergence of a subsequent disorder. Prevention, rather that treatment, must be addressed in a variety of ways. If we prevent compassion fatigue from occurring, there will be less need for treatment. Davis and Brody (1979) viewed prevention as primary, secondary, or tertiary. Primary prevention deals with causes of social problems, secondary focuses on reducing violence or preparing for its effects, and tertiary concentrates on crisis intervention in the aftermath of violence. All of these components are important and clinicians are part of the greater community. However, some types of prevention are not under the direct control of the clinician. Self-responsibility and self-care is mandatory for prevention of CT, while we all strive for prevention in the broader sense.

It is sometimes helpful for clinicians to pretend that they are giving advice to a client. What would we tell clients to do to offset stress in their lives? Frequently it is *"back to basics."* On a physical level, our recommendations would include such essentials as adequate sleep, proper nutrition, exercise, meditation, diaphragmatic breathing, relaxation, as well as numerous other health producing techniques mentioned in Chapter IV. Clinicians may also benefit from psychotherapeutic techniques such as EMDR, EFT, and resource installation. Other self-soothers include journaling, poetry, art therapy, music therapy, recreation, time management, assertiveness, and stress inoculation training. A quick review of the therapeutic techniques in Chapters Four and Five could benefit clinicians suffering from compassion fatigue.

In addition, many studies attest to the fact that humor can counteract the intensity of trauma work. Some work environments enjoy joke exchanges, where copies of jokes are placed in inboxes every day to lighten the load. Fun should be liberally applied in offices: popcorn or treats could be served during serious meetings or discussions. Breaks and lunches should be taken and restful places provided; mental health days should be offered. Institutions need to be worker-friendly and sensitive to the needs of trauma care providers.

On a personal level, clinicians may need to take a trial-and-error approach in preventing and treating compassion fatigue. With the wealth of techniques and strategies available today, clinicians can pick, choose, and discard what doesn't work, and try again. Health care professionals of all occupations possess more knowledge on treating stress-related concerns than any other group or discipline. If we would practice what we preach, much compassion fatigue could be avoided.

If we frequently assess ourselves as thoroughly and accurately as we assess our clients, we will notice the early warning signals and ward off more serious implications. Ancient Biblical scriptures have encouraged us to *"Love thy neighbor as thyself."* Behaviorally, it appears that some health care professionals have interpreted the message differently. They live as though it said, *"Love thy neighbor instead of thyself."* If we don't appropriately love and respect ourselves, then we won't be able to love and give to trauma victims. Our compassion must be big enough and broad enough to encompass ourselves and others. Let's make a *"compassion"* commitment to ourselves to maintain our physical, mental, emotional, and spiritual health, so we can continue to offer life-giving compassion to others.

# COMPASSION SATISFACTION AND FATIGUE (CSF) TEST

Helping others puts you in direct contact with other people's lives. As you probably have experienced, your compassion for those you help has both positive and negative aspects. This self-test helps you estimate your compassion status: How much at risk you are of burnout and compassion fatigue and also your degree of satisfaction with helping others. Consider each of the following characteristics about you and your current situation. Write in the number that honestly reflects how frequently you experienced these characteristics in the last week. Then follow the scoring directions at the end of the self-test.

0 = Never     1 = Rarely     2 = A few times     3 = Somewhat often
4 = Often     5 = Very often

**Items About You**

1. _____    I am happy.

2. _____    I find my life satisfying.

3. _____    I have beliefs that sustain me.

4. _____    I feel estranged from others.

5. _____    I find that I learn new things from those I care for.

6. _____    I force myself to avoid certain thoughts or feelings that remind me of a frightening experience.

7. _____    I find myself avoiding certain activities or situations because they remind me of a frightening experience.

8. _____    I have gaps in my memory about frightening events.

9. _____    I feel connected to others.

10. _____    I feel calm.

11. _____    I believe I have a good balance between my work and my free time.

12. _____    I have difficulty falling or staying asleep.

13. _____    I have outbursts of anger or irritability with little provocation.

14. _____    I am the person I always wanted to be.

15. _____    I startle easily.

16. _____    While working with a victim, I thought about violence against the perpetrator.

17. _____    I am a sensitive person.

18. _____    I have flashbacks connected to those I help.

19. _____    I have good peer support when I need to work through a highly stressful experience.

20. _____    I have had first-hand experience with traumatic events in my adult life.

21. _____    I have had first-hand experience with traumatic events in my childhood.

22. _____    I think I need to "work through" a traumatic experience in my life.

23. _____    I think I need more close friends.

24. _____    I think there is no one to talk with about highly stressful experiences.

25. _____    I have concluded that I work too hard for my own good.

26. _____    Working with those I help brings me a great deal of satisfaction.

27. _____    I feel invigorated after working with those I help.

28. _____    I am frightened of things a person I helped has said or done to me.

29. _____    I experience troubling dreams similar to those I help.

30. _____ I have happy thoughts about those I help and how I could help them.

31. _____ I have experienced intrusive thoughts of times with especially difficult people I have helped.

32. _____ I have suddenly and involuntarily recalled a frightening experience while working with a person I helped.

33. _____ I am preoccupied with more than one person I help.

34. _____ I am losing sleep over traumatic experiences of a person I help.

35. _____ I have joyful feelings about how I can help the victims with whom I work.

36. _____ I think that I might have been "infected" by the traumatic stress of those I help.

37. _____ I think that I might be positively "inoculated" by the traumatic stress of those I help.

38. _____ I remind myself to be less concerned about the well-being of those I help.

39. _____ I have felt trapped by my work as a helper.

40. _____ I have a sense of hopelessness associated with working with those I help.

41. _____ I have felt "on edge" about various things, and I attribute this to working with certain people I help.

42. _____ I wish I could avoid working with some people I help.

43. _____ Some people I help are particularly enjoyable to work with.

44. _____ I have been in danger working with people I help.

45. _____ I feel that some people I help dislike me personally.

## Items About Being a Helper and Your Helping Environment

46. _____ I like my work as a helper.

47. _____ I feel I have the tools and resources that I need to do my work as a helper.

48. _____ I have felt weak, tired, and run down as a result of my work as a helper.

49. _____ I have felt depressed as a result of my work as a helper.

50. _____ I have thoughts that I am a "success" as a helper.

51. _____ I am unsuccessful at separating helping from my personal life.

52. _____ I enjoy my coworkers.

53. _____ I depend on my coworkers to help me when I need it.

54. _____ My coworkers can depend on me for help when they need it.

55. _____ I trust my coworkers.

56. _____ I feel little compassion toward most of my coworkers.

57. _____ I am pleased with how I am able to keep up with helping technology.

58. _____ I feel I am working more for the money or prestige than for personal fulfillment.

59. _____ Although I have to do paperwork that I don't like, I still have time to work with those I help.

60. _____ I find it difficult separating my personal life from my helper life.

61. _____ I am pleased with how I am able to keep up with helping techniques and protocols.

62. _____ I have a sense of worthlessness/disillusionment/resentment associated with my role as a helper.

63. _____ I have thought that I am a "failure" as a helper.

64. _____ I have thoughts that I am not succeeding at achieving my life goals.

65. _____ I have to deal with bureaucratic, unimportant tasks in my work as a helper.

66. _____ I plan to be a helper for a long time.

## Scoring Instructions

Please note that research is ongoing on this scale, and the following scores are theoretically derived and should be used only as a guide, not as confirmatory information.

1. Be certain you respond to all items.
2. Mark the items for scoring:
   a) Put an x by the following 26 items: 1–3, 5, 9–11, 14, 19, 26–27, 30, 35, 37, 43, 46–47, 50, 52–55, 57, 59, 61, and 66.
   b) Put a check by the following 16 items: 17, 23–25, 41, 42, 45, 48, 49, 51, 56, 58, 60, and 62–65.
   c) Circle the following 23 items: 4, 6–8, 12, 13, 15, 16, 18, 20–22, 28, 29, 31–34, 36, 38–40, and 44.
3. Add the numbers you wrote next to the items for each set of items and note:
   a) *Your potential for compassion satisfaction (x):* 118 and above = extremely high potential; 100–117 = high potential; 82–99 = good potential; 64–81 = modest potential; below 63 = low potential.
   b) *Your risk for burnout (check):* 36 or less = extremely low risk; 37–50 = moderate risk; 51–75 = high risk; 76–85 = extremely high risk.
   c) *Your risk for compassion fatigue (circle):* 26 or less = extremely low risk; 27–30 = low risk; 31–35 = moderate risk; 36–40 = high risk; 41 or more = extremely high risk.

# REFERENCES

Adler, A. (1943). Neuropsychiatric complications in victims of Boston's Coconut Grove disaster. *Journal of the American Medical Association, 123*, 1098–1101.

Agency for Healthcare Research & Quality (2012). *Interventions for the prevention of post-traumatic stress disorder in adults after exposure to psychological trauma.* U.S. Department of Health and Human Services AHRQ Effective Healthcare Program, Research Protocol.

Agency for Healthcare Research & Quality (2013). *Interventions for the prevention of post-traumatic stress disorder in adults after exposure to psychological trauma.* U.S. Department of Health and Human Services AHRQ Effective Healthcare Program, Research Protocol.

Allen, J.C. (1995). *Coping with trauma: A guide to self-understanding.* Washington, DC: American Psychiatric Press, Inc.

Amen, Daniel G. (1998). *Change your brain, change your life: The breakthrough program for conquering anxiety, depression, obsessiveness, anger, and impulsiveness.* New York: Random House.

American Psychological Association (2013). *The APA dictionary of clinical psychology.* Washington, D.C., Gary R. Vandenbos, editor.

American Psychiatric Association. (2000). *Diagnostic and Statistical Manual of Mental Disorders,* (4th ed., text revision). (2000). Washington, DC: American Psychiatric Association.

American Psychiatric Association. (2013). *Diagnostic and statistical manual of mental disorders* (5th ed.). Washington, D.C.: American Psychiatric Association.

Armitage, R., Ruch, A.J., Trivedi, M., Cain, J., & Roffwarg, H.P. (1994). The effects of nefazodone on sleep architecture in depression. *Neuropsychopharmacology 10*, 123–127.

Baranowsky, A.B. (2002). The Silencing Response in Clinical Practice: On the Road to Dialogue. In C.R. Figley (Ed.), *Treating compassion fatigue.* New York: Brunner-Routledge.

Beck, A.T. (1976). *Cognitive therapy and the emotional disorders.* New York: University Press.

Benson, H. (1975). *The relaxation response.* New York: William Morrow & Co..

Blank, A.S. (1993). The longitudinal course of post-traumatic stress disorder. In J.R.T. Davidson, & E.B.Foa (Eds.) *Post-traumatic stress disorder: DSM-IV and beyond,* (pp.3–22), Washington, DC: American Psychiatric Press.

Bonhoeffer, M. (1926). Beurteilung, begutachtung, und rechtsprechung bei den sogenanaten unfollsneuroson. *Deutsche Medizinische Wochenschrife, 52*, 179–182.

Bowlby, J. (1980a). Attachment and loss, Vol. 3: Loss, sadness and depression. New York: Basic Books.

Brady, K., Pearlstein, T., Asnis G.M., Baker, D., Rothbaum, B., Sikes, C.R., et al. (2000). Efficacy and safety of sertraline treatment of posttraumatic stress disorder: A randomized controlled trial. *Journal of the American Medical Association, 283*, 1837–1844.

Brady, K.T., Sonne, S.C., & Roberts, J.M. (1995). Sertraline treatment of comorbid posttraumatic stress disorder and alcohol dependence. *Journal of Clinical Psychiatry, 56*, 502–505.

Bremner, J.D. (2002). *Does stress damage the brain?* New York: W. W. Norton & Co.

Bremner, J.D., Vermetten, E., & Mazure, C.M. (2000). Development and preliminary psychometric properties of an instrument for the measurement of childhood trauma: The Early Trauma Inventory. *Depression and Anxiety, 12*, 1–12.

Bremner, J.D., Randall, P., Scott, T.M., Bronen, R.A., Seibyl, J.P., Southwick, S.M., et al. (1995). MRI-based measurement of hippocampal volume in posttraumatic stress disorder. *American Journal of Psychiatry, 152*, 973–981.

Bremner, J.D., Randall, P.R., Capelli, S., Scott, T., McCarthy, G., & Charney, D.S. (1995). Deficits in short-term memory in adult survivors of childhood abuse. *Psychiatry Research, 59*, 97–107.

Bremner, J.D., Randall, P., Vermetten, E., Staib, L., Bronen, R.A., Capelli, S., et al. (1997). "MRI-based measurement of hippocampal volume in posttraumatic stress disorder related to childhood physical and sexual abuse: A preliminary report." *Biological Psychiatry, 41*, 23–32.

Bremner, J.D., Narayan, M., Anderson, E.R., Staib, L.H., Miller, H., & Charney, D.S. (2000). Hippocampal volume reduction in major depression. *American Journal of Psychiatry, 157*, 115–117.

Brewin, C.R., Andrews, B., Rose, S., & Kirk, M. (1999). Acute stress disorder and posttraumatic stress disorder in victims of violent crime. *American Journal of Psychiatry, 156*, 360–366.

Brickner, Sheryl (1999). "Emotional Freedom Techniques." *CoACCT Newsletter* 8-3-99.

Briere, J. (1996). *Therapy for adults molested as children beyond survival, 2nd edition*, New York: Springer Publishing Company.

Briere, J. (1997). *Psychological assessment of adult posttraumatic states*, Washington, DC: American Psychological Association.

Briere, J. (2004). *Psychological assessment of adult posttraumatic states: Phenomenology, diagnosis, and measurement (2nd ed.)*. Washington, DC: American Psychological Association.

Briere, J., & Scott, C. (2006). *Principles of trauma therapy: A guide to symptoms, evaluation, and treatment*. Thousand Oaks, CA: Sage Publications.

Bucci, W. (2002). The referential process, consciousness, and the sense of self. *Psychoanalytic Inquiry, 5*, 766-793.

Cannon, W.B. (1914). The emergency function of the adrenal medulla in pain and the major stress emotions. *American Journal of Physiology, 3*, 356–372.

Cannon, W.B. (1927). The James-Lange theory of emotions: A critical reappraisal and alternative theory. *Journal of Psychology, 39*, 106–124.

Cohen J.A., Mannarino, A.P. & Deblinger, E. (2006). *Treating trauma and traumatic grief in children and adolescents,* New York: The Guilford Press.

Corrigan, F., Fisher, J.J. & Nutt, D. (2011). Affect dysregulation and the Window of Tolerance model of the effects of complex trauma. *Journal of Psychopharmacology, 25,*17-25.

Courtois, C.A. & Ford, J.D. (Eds.). (2009). *Treating complex traumatic stress disorders: An evidence-based guide.* New York: The Guilford Press.

Courtois, C.A. & Ford, J.D. (2013). *Treatment of complex trauma: A sequenced, relationship-based approach.* New York: The Guilford Press.

Craig, G., & Fowlie, A. (1995). *Emotional freedom techniques: The manual.* The Sea Ranch, CA.

Danielli, Y. (1984). Psychotherapists' participation in the conspiracy of silence about the Holocaust. *Psychoanalytic Psychology, 1,* 23–42.

Davidson, J.H., Kudler, H., Smith, R. et al. (1990). Treatment of post-traumatic stress disorder with amitryptyline and placebo. *Archives of General Psychiatry, 47,* 259–266.

Davidson, J.R.T., Malik, M.L., & Sutherland, S.M. (1996). Response characteristics to antidepressants and placebo in post-traumatic stress disorder. *International Clinical Psychopharmacology, 12,* 291–296.

Davidson, J. & van der Kolk, B. (1996). The psychopharmacological treatment of posttraumatic stress disorder. In B.A. van der Kolk, A.C. McFarlane, & L. Weisaeth (Eds.) *Traumatic stress: The effects of overwhelming experience on mind, body, and society* (pp. 510–524). New York: Guilford Press.

Davis, M. (1992). The role of the amygdala in fear and anxiety. *Annual Reviews of Neuroscience, 15,* 353–375.

Davis, L.J. & Brody, E.W. (1979). Rape and older women: A guide to preventional protection. U.S. Department of Health and Welfare, National Institute of Mental Health, DHHS Publication No. ADM 78–734.

DeBoer, M.C., Opden Velde, W., Falger, P.R.J., Hovens, J.E., DeGroen, J.H.M., & Van Duijn, H. (1992). Fluvoxamine treatment for chronic PTSD: A pilot study. *Psychotherapy and Psychosomatics, 57,* 158–163.

Ellis, A. (1962). *Reason and emotion in psychotherapy,* New York: Stuart Press.

Felitti V.J., Anda R.F., Nordernberg D., etal. (1998). Relationship of childhood abuse to many of the leading causes of death in adults: the adverse childhood experiences (ACE) study. *American Journal of Preventive Medicine. 14*(4): 245-258.

Figley, C.R., & Carbonell, J. (1995). The 'Active Ingredient' Project: The systematic clinical demonstration of the most efficient treatments of PTSD, a research plan. Tallahassee: Florida State University Psychosocial Stress Research Program and Clinical Laboratory, in Gallo, F (Ed.) *Energy Psychology.* Washington, DC: CRC Press.

Figley, C.R. (1995). *Compassion fatigue: Coping with secondary traumatic stress disorder in those who treat the traumatized,* New York: Brunner/Mazel.

Figley, C.R., & Stamm, B.H. (1996). Psychometric Review of the Compassion Fatigue Self-Test. In B.H. Stamm (Ed.), *Measurement of stress, trauma and adaptation,* Lutherville, MD: Sidran Press.

Figley, C.R. (2002). *Treating compassion fatigue,* New York: Brunner/Mazel.

First, M.B., Spitzer, R.L., Gibbon, M., Williams, J. (1997). *SCID-1 Administration Booklet,* American Psychiatric Press, Inc.

Fisher, J. (2008). *Starting from the child* (3rd ed.).New York: Open University Press.

Fisher, J. (2010). Brain to brain. *Psychotherapy Networker,* January 2010.

Fisher, J. (2011). Attachment from a sensorimotor perspective. *Attachment: New Directions in Psychotherapy and Relational Psychoanalysis.*

Fisher, J. (2011). Sensorimotor approaches to trauma treatment. *Advances in Psychiatric Treatment, 17*:171-177.

Fisher, J. (2011). "Breaking free: A mind-body approach to retraining the brain. *Psychotherapy Networker,* March 2011.

Fisher, J. (2011). *Psychoeducational aids for the treatment of psychological trauma.* Cambridge, MA: Kendell Press.

Fisher, J & Ogden, P. (2009). Sensorimotor psychotherapy. In C. Courtois & J. Ford (Eds.), *Treating complex-traumatic stress disorders,* New York: Wiley & Sons.

Foa, E.B., Davidson, J.R.T., & Frances, A. (1999). The expert consensus guideline series: Treatment of posttraumatic stress disorder, *Journal of Clinical Psychiatry, 60* (Suppl. 16), 1–18.

Foa, E.B. (2011). The cutting edge prolonged exposure therapy: Past, present, and future. *Depression and Anxiety, 28*: 1043-1047.

Frankl, V. (1959). *From death camp to existent lives.* New York: Beacon Press.

Frankl, V. (1984). *Man's search for meaning* (3rd Ed.). New York: Pocket Books.

French, G.D., & Harris, C.J. (1998). *Traumatic incident reduction,* Boca Raton, FL: CRC Press LLC.

Freud, S. (1955). *Beyond the pleasure principle* (pp.29–33). Standard Edition, Vol. 18, (original work published 1920), London: Hogarth Press.

Friedman, M.J. & Southwick, S.M. (1995). Towards pharmacotherapy for PTSD. In M.J. Friedman, D.S. Charney & A.Y. Deutch (Eds.), *Neurobiologic and clinical consequences of stress: From normal adaptation to PTSD* (pp. 465–481). Philadelphia, PA: Lippincott-Raven Press.

Friedman, M.J. (1990). Interrelationships between biological mechanisms and pharmacotherapy of posttraumatic stress disorder. In M.E. Wolfe & A.D. Mosnaim (Eds.), *Post-Traumatic Stress Disorder: Etiology, Phenomenology, and Treatment* (pp. 204–225). Washington, DC: American Psychiatric Press.

Friedman, M.J. (2001). *Post-traumatic stress disorder: The latest assessment and treatment strategies.* Kansas City, MO: Dean Psych. Press Corp.

Gainotti, G. (2000). Neuropsychological theories of emotion. In J. Borod (Ed.) *The neuropsychology of emotion*. New York: Oxford University Press.

Gentry, Eric J. (2002). *Instructional manual* (Version 4.3). Tampa FL: Traumatology Institute.

Geschwind, N. & Galaburda, A. (1987). *Cerebral lateralization: biological mechanisms, associations and pathology*. Boston: MIT Press.

Gould, E., Tanapat, P., McEwen, B.S., Flugge, G., & Fuchs, E. (1998). Proliferation of granule cell precursors in the dentate gyrus of adult monkeys is diminished by stress. *Proceedings of the National Academy of Sciences USA, 95*, 3168–3171.

Guralnik, D.B. (1970). *Webster's new world dictionary of the American language*. Nashville, TN: The World Publishing Co.

Hansen, D. (2014). *An update on nutritional supplementation for the prevention and treatment of PTSD*. Littleton, CO.

Hearst, P.C. & Moscow, A. (1982). *Every secret thing*, New York: Doubleday.

Henry, J.P. (1993). Psychological and physiological responses to stress: The right hemisphere and the hypothalamo-pituitary-adrenal axis, an inquiry into problems of human bonding. *Integrative Physiological and Behavioral Science, 28.* 4, 369-387.

Herman, J.L. (1992). *Trauma and recovery*. New York: Basic Books.

Herman, J.L. (2009). *Treating complex traumatic stress disorders an evidence-based guide*. In: C.A. Courtois and J.D. Ford (Eds.), NY: Guilford Press.

Herman, J.L. (2012). Why is some trauma complex? A helpful distinction from Judith Herman. Accessed 12/1/2014 at: http://wisecounsel.wordpress.com/2012/04/24/why-is-some-trauma-complex-a-helpful-distinction-from-judith-herman/

Hilberman, E. (1980). The 'wife-beater's wife' reconsidered. *Am. J. Psychiatry, 137*, 1336–1347.

Hobson, J.A. (1994). *The chemistry of conscious states: How the brain changes its mind*. Boston: Little, Brown & Co.

Horowitz, M. (1986). *Stress response syndromes*. New York, NY: Jason Aronson.

Horowitz, M. (1999). *Essential papers on posttraumatic stress disorder*, New York: University Press.

Hudgins, K.M. (2002). *Experiential treatments for PTSD:, The therapeutic spiral model*. New York: Springer Publishing Co., Inc.

Inman, D.J., Silver, S.M & Doghramji, K. (1990). Sleep disturbance in post-traumatic stress disorder: A comparison with non-PTSD insomnia. *Journal of Traumatic Stress 3*, 429–437.

Institute for American Values, (2003). *Hardwired to Connect: the new scientific case for authoritative communities, executive summary*, Accessed 12/1/2014 at: http://www.americanvalues.org/html/hardwired_-_ex_summary.html. Words run together - can't correct

Jacobs, T. J. (1994). Nonverbal communications: Some reflections on their role in the psychoanalytic process and psychoanalytic education. *Journal of the American Psychoanalytic Association. 42*, 741-762.

Jacobs, S. C. (1999). *Traumatic grief: Diagnosis, treatment, and prevention.* Castleton, NY: Hamilton Printing Co.

Joinson, C. (1992). Coping with compassion fatigue. *Nursing, 22* (4), 116–122.

Keane, T., Fairbank, J., Caddell, J., Zimering, R., Taylor, K., & Mora, C. (1989). Combat Exposure Scale (CES) Clinical evaluation of a measure to assess combat exposure. *Psychological Assessment, 1*, 53-55.

Kernberg, O. (1967). Borderline personality organization. *Journal of the American Psychoanalyti. Asso*ciation, *15*, 641–685.

Kessler, R.C., Sonnega, A., Bromet, E., Hughes, M., & Nelson, C.B. (1995). Posttraumatic stress disorder in the national comorbidity survey. *Archives of General Psychiatry, 52*, 1048–1060.

Kinney, H.C., Brody, B.A., Kloman, A.S. & Giles, F.H. (1988). Sequence of central nervous system myelination in human infancy II Patterns of myelination in autopsied infants. *Journal of Neuropathology and Experimental Neurology. 47*, 217 – 234.

Kinzie, J.D. & Leung, P. (1989). Clonidine in Cambodian patients with posttraumatic stress disorder. *Journal of Nervous and Mental Disease, 177*, 546–550.

Kolb, L.C., Burris, B.C., & Griffiths, S. (1984). Propranolol and clonidine in the treatment of the chronic post-traumatic stress disorders of war. In B.A. van der Kolk (Ed.), *Post-traumatic stress disorder: psychological and biological sequelae* (pp. 97–107). Washington, DC: American Psychiatric Press.

Kramer, M.S., Schoen, L.S., & Kinney, L. (1984). The dream experience in dream disturbed Vietnam veterans. In *Post-traumatic Stress Disorders: Psychological and Biological Sequelae.* B. van der Kolk (Ed.), Washington, DC: American Psychiatric Press.

Krystal, H. (Ed.) (1968). *Massive psychic trauma.* New York: International Universities Press.

Lazarus, R. (1984). Puzzles in the study of daily hassles. *Journal of Behavioral Medicine. 7*: 375–389.

Le Chapman, W.P., Schroeder, H.R., Guyer, G., Brazier, M.A.B., Fager, C., Poppen, J.L., et al. (1954). Physiological evidence concerning the importance of the amygdaloid nuclear region in the integration of circulating functions and emotion in man. *Science, 729*, 949–950.

LeDoux, J.E. (1993). Emotional memory systems in the brain. *Behavioral and Brain Research, 58*, 69–79.

Leeds, A.M. (1999). "Principles of case formulation and use of EMDR Resource Development and installation in the treatment of complex posttraumatic stress disorder and adults with insecure attachment status." EMDR Institute: Level 2 Specialty Presentation, Denver, CO.

Lerner, Mark D. (2001). *An overview of experts in traumatic stress, trauma response.* New York: The American Academy of Experts in Traumatic Stress, Inc., www.aaets.org.

Lifton, R. J., & Olson, E. (1976). Death imprint in Buffalo Creek. In H. J. Parad, H. L. P. Resnik, & L. G. Parad (Eds.), *Emergency and disaster management: A mental health sourcebook* (pp. 295-308). Bowie, MD: The Charles Press.

Lin PY, Huang SY, & Su KP (2011). A meta-analytic review of polyunsaturated fatty acid compositions in patients with depression *Biological Psychiatry, 68*: 140-147.

Lindemann, E. (1944). "Symptomatology and management of acute grief." *American Journal Psychiatry, 101*: 141–148.

Lindy, J.D. (1985). The trauma membrane and other concepts derived from psychotherapeutic work with survivors of natural disaster. *Psychiatric Annals, 15* (3), 153–160.

Lindy, J.D. (1996). Psychoanalytic psychotherapy of post-traumatic stress disorder: The nature of the therapeutic relationship. In B. van der Kolk, A. McFarlane, & L. Weisaeth (Eds.) *Traumatic stress: The effects of overwhelming experience on mind, body, and society* (pp. 525–536), New York: Guilford Press.

Lindy, J.D., & Wilson, J.P. (2001). "Respecting the trauma membrane: Above all, do no harm." In: *Treating psychological trauma & PTSD.* Wilson, J.P., Friedman, M.J., & Lindy, J.D. (Eds.). New York: Guilford Press.

Linehan, M.M. (1993). *Cognitive-behavioral treatment of borderline personality disorder.* New York: Guilford Press.

Lovelace, L., & McGrady, M. (1980). *Ordeal,* Secaucus, NJ: Citadel.

Mandal & Pearlman, L.A. (1990). Vicarious traumatization: A framework for understanding the psychological effects of working with victims. *Journal of Traumatic Stress, 3* (1), 131–150.

Mandal, M.K. & Ambady, N. (2004). Laterality of facial expressions of emotion: Universal and culture-specific influences, *Behavioral Neurology, 15*, 23-34.

Maslach, C. (1982). *Burnout: The Cost of Caring.* Englewood Cliffs, N.J.: Prentice-Hall.

Matsuoka Y, Nishi D, Yonemoto N, Hamazaki K, Hamazaki T, & Hashimoto K (2010). Omega-3 fatty acids for secondary prevention of posttraumatic stress disorder after accidental injury: An open-label pilot study. *Journal of Clinical Psychopharmacology, 30*, 217-219.

Matsuoka Y, Nishi D, Yonemoto N, Hamazaki K, Hamazaki T, & Hashimoto K (2011). Potential role of BDNF in the omega-3 fatty acid supplementation to prevent posttraumatic distress after accidental injury: An open-label pilot study. *Psychotherapy and Psychosomatics, 80*, 310-312.

Matsuoka Y, Nishi D, Yonemoto N, Hamazaki K, Matsumura K, Noguchi H, et al. (2013). Tachikawa project for prevention of posttraumatic stress disorder with polyunsaturated fatty acid (TPOP): Study protocol for a randomized controlled trial. *BMC Psychiatry 13*:8.

McCann, I.L., & Pearlman, L.A. (1990). Vicarious traumatization: A framework for understanding the psychological effects of working with victims. *Journal of Traumatic Stress, 3*, 131–150.

McEwen, B.S., Angulo, J., Cameron, H., Chao, H.M., Daniels, D., Gannon, M.N., et al. (1992). Paradoxical effects of adrenal steroids on the brain: Protection versus degeneration. *Biological Psychiatry, 31*, 177–199.

McEwen, B.S., Conrad, C.D., Kuroda, Y., Frankfurt, M., Magarinos, A.M., & McKittrick, C. (1997). Prevention of stress-induced morphological and cognitive consequences. *European Neuropsychopharmacology, 7* (3), 322–328.

McFarlane, A.C., Weber, D.L., & Clark, C.R. (1993). Abnormal stimulus processing in post-traumatic stress disorder. *Biological Psychiatry, 34*, 311–320.

Mellman, T.A., Kulick-Bell, R., Ashlock, L.E. & Nolan, B (1995). Sleep events in combat-related post traumatic stress disorder. *American Journal of Psychiatry, 152*, 110–115.

National Institutes of Health (2013). Clinical trials University Hospital, Toulouse, ClinicalTrials. gov.identifier

Niederland, W.G. (1968). Clinical observations on the 'survivor syndrome.' *International Journal of Psychoanalysis, 49*, 313–315.

Nuland, Sherwin B. (1995, 2010). *How we die: Reflections on life's final chapter.* New York: Vintage Books.

Ogden, P., Minton, K. (2000). Sensorimotor psychotherapy: One method for processing trauma. *Traumatology,* 6 Retrieved from: www.fse.edu/trauma/v6i3a3.html.

Ogden, P., Minton, K. & Pain, C. (2006). *Trauma and the body: A sensorimotor approach to psychotherapy.* New York: W.W. Norton.

Osmani, S. & Sen, A. (2003). The hidden penalties of gender inequality: fetal origins of ill-health. *Economics and Human Biology 1,* 1, 105-121.

Pennebaker, J.W. & Campbell, R.S. (2000). The effects of writing about traumatic experience. *Clinical Quarterly* 9(2): *17,* 19–21.

Perls, F.S. (1969). *Gestalt therapy verbatim,* Moab, UT: Real People Press.

Perry, B.D. (1994). Neurobiological sequelae of childhood trauma: Post traumatic stress disorders in children. In M. Murburg (Ed.), *Catecholamines in posttraumatic stress disorder: Emerging concepts* (pp. 233–276). Washington, DC: American Psychiatric Press.

Pert, C. (1997). *Molecules of emotion: Why you feel the way you feel,* New York: Scribner.

Porges, S.W. (1995). *Cardiac vagal tone: a physiological index of stress,* Neuroscience and Biobehavioral Reviews, 19, 225-233

Porges, S.W. (2001a). The polyvagal theory: Phylogenetic substates of a social nervous system. *International Journal of Psychophysiology, 42*, 123-146.

Porges, S.W. (2001b). Is there a major stress system at the periphery other than the adrenals? In D.M. Broom (Ed.), *Dahlem workshop on coping with challenge: welfare in animals including humans.* Berlin: Dahlem University Press.

Porges, S.W. (2004). Neuroception: a subconscious system for detecting threats and safety. Zeroto three.org.

Porges, S. W. (2008, February). *The Perspective.* NIH Public Access, PMC1868418.

Porges, S.W. (2005). The role of social engagement in attachment and bonding: A phylogenetic perspective. In Carter, C.S. et al. (Eds.). *Attachment and bonding: A new synthesis.* Cambridge, MA: MIT Press.

Porges, S.W. (2011). *The polyvagal theory.* New York: W. W. Norton & Company.

Prigerson, H.G., Shear, M.K., Jacobs, S.C., Reynolds, C.F. III, Maciejewski, J.R., Davidson, J.R.T., et al. (1999). Consensus criteria for traumatic grief: A preliminary empirical test. *British Journal of Psychiatry, 194*, 67–73.

Prigerson, H.G., Maciejewski, P.K., Newsom, J., Reynolds, C.F., Frank, E., Bierhals, A.J.,. (1995). The Inventory of Complicated Grief: A scale to measure maladaptive symptoms of loss. *Psychiatry Research, 59*, 65–79.

Prigerson, H. G., Vanderwerker, L. C., & Maciejewski, P. K. (2007). Prolonged grief disorder: Inclusion in DSM complicated grief as a mental disorder. *Handbook of bereavement research and practice: 21st century perspectives,* M.Stroebe R.Hansson, H. Schut & W. Stroebe (Eds.), Washington, D.C.: American Psychological Association Press.

Putnam, F.W., et al. (1986). The clinical phenomenology of multiple personality disorder: A review of 100 recent cases. *Journal of Clinical psychiatry, 47*, 283–293.

Rando, T.A. (1993). *Treatment of Complicated Mourning,* Champaign, IL: Research Press.

Raphael, B., & Wilson, J.P. (2000). Psychotherapeutic and pharmacology intervention for bereaved persons". *Handbook of bereavement research and practice.* Washington, DC: American Psychiatric Association.

Reber, A.S. (2009). *The penguin dictionary of psychology* (4th Ed.) London, England: Penguin Group.

Remer, R. & Elliot, J. (1988). Management of secondary victims of sexual assault. *International Journal of Family Psychiatry, 9* (4), 389–400.

Resick, P.A. (2001). *Stress and trauma.* Philadelphia, PA: Psychology Press.

Resick, P.A.& Schnicke, M.K. (1993). *Cognitive processing therapy for rape victims: A treatment manual.* Thousand Oaks, CA: Sage.

Resick, P.A., et al. (2012). A critical evaluation of the complex PTSD literature: Implications for DSM-5. *Journal of Traumatic Stress, 25*, 241-251.

Resnick, H. S., Falsetti, S. A., Kilpatrick, D. G., & Freedy, J. R. (1996). Potential Stressful Experiences Inventory (PSEI), National Center for PTSD at www.ptsd.va.gov.

Reynolds, C.F., Buysse, D.J., Kupper, D.J., Hoch, C.C., Houch, P.R., Matzzie, J., et al.. (1990). Rapid eye movement sleep deprivation as probe in elderly subjects. *Archives of General Psychiatry 47*, 1128–1136.

Rieker, P.P. & Carmen, E. (1986). The victim-to-patient process: The disconfirmation and transformation of abuse." *American Journal of Orthopsychiatry. 56*, 360–370.

Ross, R.J., Ball, W.A., Dinges, D.F., Kribbs, N.B., Morrison, A.R., Silver, S.M., et al.(1994). Rapid eye movement sleep disturbance in posttraumatic stress disorder. *Biological Psychiatry 35*, 195–202.

Sanders, B., & Becker-Lausen, E. (1995). The measurement of psychological maltreatment: Early data on the Child Abuse and Trauma Scale. Child Abuse and Neglect, *19*, 315-323.

Scaer, R. C. (2001). *The body bears the burden: Trauma, dissociation, and disease.* Binghamton, NY: The Hawthorne Press.

Scaer, R. C. (2005). *The trauma spectrum: Hidden wounds and human resiliency.* New York: Norton Publishers.

Sapolsky, R.M. (1996). Why stress is bad for your brain. *Science, 273,* 749–750.

Schore, A. (1994). Affect regulation and the origin of self: The neurobiology of emotional development. Hillsdale, NJ: Lawrence Erlbaum Associates .

Schore, A. (2002). Dysregulation of the right brain: A fundamental mechanism of traumatic attachment and the psychopathogenesis of post-traumatic stress disorder. *Australian and New Zealand Journal of Psychiatry, 36,* 9-30.

Schore, A. (2003). *Affect regulation, and the repair of the self.* New York: Norton Publishers.

Schore, A.N. (2005). "Attachment, affect regulation and the developing right brain: linking developmental neuroscience to pediatrics" *Pediatrics in Review, 26,* (6), 204-217.

Schore, A.N. (2007). Review of *Awakening the dreamer: clinical journeys* by Philip M. Bromberg, *Psychoanalytic Dialogues, 17,* 753-767.

Schore, A. (2010). Relational trauma and the developing right brain: The neurobiology of broken attachment bonds. In: T. Baradon, (Ed.).Relational trauma in infancy: Psychoanalytic, attachment and neuropsychological contributions to parent–infant psychotherapy. (pp. 19-47). New York: Routledge/Taylor & Francis Group.

Schore, A. (2009). Relational trauma and the developing right brain: Origins of pathological dissociation. *Annals of the New York Academy of Sciences, 1159,* 189-203.

Schore, J. & Schore, A. (2007). *Modern attachment theory: The central role of affect regulation in development and treatment.* Springer Science + Business Media, LLC.

Schupp, Linda J. (1992). *Is there life after loss?* Lakewood, CO.

Schupp, Linda J. (2003). *Grief: Normal, complicated, and traumatic.* Eau Claire, WI: PESI, LLC.

Seaward, B.L. (1999). *Managing stress: Principles and strategies for health and well-being.* (2nd Ed.). Boston: Jones and Bartlett Publishers.

Selye, H. (1976). *The stress of life.* New York: McGraw-Hill. Selye, H. (1956). *The stress of life..* New York, McGraw-Hill Book Company, Inc.

Shalev, Arieh Y. (1996). Stress versus traumatic stress: From acute homeostatic reactions to chronic psychopathology. In B.A. van der Kolk, A.C. McFarlane, & L. Weisaeth (Eds.) *Traumatic stress: The effects of overwhelming experience on mind, body, and society,* (pp. 83–85), New York: Guilford Press.

Shapiro, F. (1989). Eye movement desensitization: A new treatment for post traumatic stress disorder. *Journal of Behavior Therapy and Experimental Psychiatry, 20,* 211–217.

Shapiro, F. (1995). *Eye movement desensitization and reprocessing: Basic principles, protocols, and procedures.* New York: Guilford Press.

Shapiro, F. (1998). *EMDR level I training manual. Pacific Grove*, CA: EMDR Institute.

Sheline, Y., Wang, P., Gado, M., Csernansky, J., & Vannier, M. (1996). Hippocampal atrophy in major depression. *Proceedings of the National Academy of Sciences: USA, 93*, 3908–3913.

Shepard, M.F. & Campbell, J.A. (1992). The abusive behavior inventory: A measure of psychological and physical abuse. *Journal of Interpersonal Violence, 7*, (3), 291–305. Inventory - pages 303–304.

Shuren, J.E. & Grafman, J. (2002). The neurology of reasoning. *Archives of Neurology. 59*, 916-919.

Sieratzki J. S., Woll B. (1996). Why do mothers cradle their babies on the left? *Lancet 347* 1746–1748 10.1016. Pub Med.

Sigman, M., & Siegel, D.J. (1992). The interface between the psychobiological and cognitive models of attachment. *Behavioral and Brain Sciences, 15*, (3), 523.

Siegel, B. (1986). *Love, medicine, & miracles*, New York: Harper & Row.

Siegel, D.J. (1999). *The development of the mind: toward a neurobiology of interpersonal experience*. New York: Guilford Press.

Siegel, D.J. (2010). *Mindsight: The science of personal transformation*. New York: Random House.

Sime, W.E, (1984). *Psychological benefits of exercise training in the healthy individual. In J.D. Mazzaro, S.M. Weiss, S.M. Herd et al. (Eds.). Behavioral health: A handbook of health enhancement and disease prevention (*pp. 488–508). New York: John Wiley & Sons.

Smith, M.A., Makino, S., Kvetnansky, R., & Post, R.M. (1995). Stress and glucocorticoids affect the expression of brain-derived neurotrophic factor and neurotrophin-e mRNA in the hippocampus. *Journal of Neuroscience, 15*, 1768–1777.

Stein, M.B., Koverola, C., Hanna, C., Torchia, M.G., & McClarty, B. (1997). Hippocampal volume in women victimized by childhood sexual abuse. *Psychological Medicine, 27*, 951–959.

Stierlin, E. (1911). Nervose und psychische stoning nach katastrophen (Nervous and psychic disturbances after catastrophes) *Deutsches Medizinische Worhenschrift, 37*, 2028–2035.

Southwick, S.M., Yehuda, R., Giller, E., et al. (1994). Use of tricyclics and monoamine oxidase inhibitors in the treatment of PTSD: A quantitative review. M.M. Murburg (Ed.), *Catecholamine function in post-traumatic stress disorder: Emerging concepts* (pp. 293–305). Washington, DC: American Psychiatry Press.

Terr, L. (1994). *Unchained memories: True stories of traumatic memories lost and found*, New York: Basic Books.

The World Mental Health (2004). Composite International Diagnostic Interview (CIDI), www.hcp.med.harvard.edu/wmhcidi/about.php

Thomas, C.B., Duszynski, K.R.,(1974). Closeness to parents and the family constellation in a prospective study of five disease states: suicide, mental illness, malignant tumor, hypertension, and coronary heart disease, *Johns Hopkins Medical Journal, 134*, no. 5.

Thompson, R. & Smith, C. (1993, May/June). "Trauma touch therapy", *Massage Magazine.*

Timerman, J. (1981). *Prisoner without a name, cell without a number,* (Trans. Talbot, T.), New York: Vintage Press.

Tucker, D.M. (1992). Development of emotions and cortical networks. In M.R. Gunnar (Ed.). *Mental behavioral neuroscience.* Hillsdale, NJ: Lawrence Erlbaum Associates.

Tutte, J.C. (2004). The concept of physical trauma: a bridge in interdisciplinary space. *International Journal of Psychoanalysis. 85,* 897-921.

Uno, H., Tarara, R., Else, J.G., Suleman, M.A., & Sapolsky, R.M. (1989). Hippocampal damage associated with prolonged and fatal stress in primates. *Journal of Neuroscience, 9,* 1705–1711.

van der Kolk, B.A. (1987). *Psychological trauma.* Washington, DC: American Psychiatric Press.

van der Kolk, B.A., (2005). Developmental Trauma Disorder. Psychiatric Annals *35*:5,

van der Kolk, B.A. (2011). Foreword in Stephen W. Porges' *The Polyvagal Theory.*

van der Kolk, B.A. (2013). Interview by Linda Curran for current PTSD treatments.

van der Kolk, B.A., & Ducey, C. (1989). The psychological processing of traumatic experience: Rorschach patterns in PTSD. *Journal of Traumatic Stress, 2,* 259–274.

van der Kolk, B.A., Dryfuss, D., Michaels, M., Berkowitz, R., Saxe, G., & Goldenberg, I. (1994). Fluoxetine in post-traumatic stress disorder. *Journal of Clinical Psychiatry, 55,* 517–522.

van der Kolk, B.A. & Fisler, R. (1995). Dissociation and the fragmentary nature of traumatic memories. Overview and exploratory study. *Journal of Traumatic Stress, 9,* 505–525.

van der Kolk, B.A., McFarlane, A.C., Weisaeth, W. (1996). *Traumatic stress,* New York, NY: The Guilford Press.

van der Kolk, B.A., Burbridge, J.A., & Suzuki, J. (1997). The psychobiology of traumatic memory. *Annals New York Academy of Science,* 99–110.

Weathers, F.W., Blake, D.D., Schnurr, P.P., Kaloupek, D.G., Marx, B.P., & Keane, T.M. (2013). The Clinician-Administered PTSD Scale for DSM-5 (CAPS-5). Interview available from the National Center for PTSD. Retrieved from: www.ptsd.va.gov.

Westerlund, E. (1992). *Women's sexuality after childhood incest,* New York: W. W. Norton.

Wilbarger, P. & Wilbarger, J. (1997). *Sensory defensiveness and related social/emotional and neurological problems.* Van Nuys, CA: Wilbarger.

Williams, M.B. & Poijula, S. (2002). *The PTSD workbook: Simple, effective techniques for overcoming traumatic stress,* Oakland, CA: New Harbinger Publications, Inc..

Wolfe, Jessica, Brown, Pamela J., Furey, Joan; Levin, Karen B. (1993). *Psychological Assessment, 5*(3), 330-335.

Yehuda, R., & McFarlane, A.C. (1995). Conflict between current knowledge about posttraumatic stress disorder and its original conceptual basis. *American Journal of Psychiatry, 152,* 1705–1713.